Blades, Bands, and Ballers

How "Flash and Cash" Rescued the Flyers and Created Philadelphia's Greatest Showplace

A Memoir by

Lou Scheinfeld

D1548065

Camino Books, Inc.
Philadelphia

Manufactured in the United States of America
1 2 3 4   24 23 22 21

Library of Congress Cataloging-in-Publication Data

Names: Scheinfeld, Lou, author.
Title: Blades, bands, and ballers : how "Flash and Cash" rescued the flyers and created
   Philadelphia's greatest showplace: a memoir by Lou Scheinfeld / Lou Scheinfeld.
Description: Philadelphia : Camino Books, Inc., 2021.
Identifiers: LCCN 2021025500 (print) | LCCN 2021025501 (ebook) | ISBN
   9781680980479 (paperback) | ISBN 9781680980486 (ebook)
Subjects: LCSH: Scheinfeld, Lou. | Snider, Edward, 1933-2016. | Sports executives—United
States—Biography. | Philadelphia Flyers (Hockey team)—History. | Hockey—Pennsylvania—
Philadelphia—History. | Arenas—Pennsylvania—Philadelphia—History. | National Hockey
   League—History.
Classification: LCC GV697.S34 A3 2021 (print) | LCC GV697.S34 (ebook) |
   DDC 796.962/640974811—dc23
LC record available at https://lccn.loc.gov/2021025500
LC ebook record available at https://lccn.loc.gov/2021025501

Cataloging-in-Publication data available from the Library of Congress, Washington, DC.

ISBN 978-1-68098-047-9
ISBN 978-1-68098-048-6 (ebook)

Cover and interior design: Jerilyn DiCarlo

This book is available at a special discount on bulk purchases for educational, business, and promotional purposes. For information write:

Publisher
Camino Books, Inc.
P.O. Box 59026
Philadelphia, PA 19102

www.caminobooks.com

Dedicated to

Ed Snider

Ed knew business.

I knew Philly.

I swear everything you're going to read

is 100 percent true and accurate—

at least as I remember it.

Contents

Foreword

Lou Scheinfeld and I met on the field of battle, directing foot soldiers in the belly of a gravel pit. But my battalion was made of plastic; his were real. I was rising to 3rd grade; Lou, a new pay grade. I was 8 years old; Lou was all of 28. It was 1964. Soon the steel skeletal frame of a yet unnamed modern arena would rise from the dust, casting a long silhouette in the night sky over South Philadelphia.

Only a year earlier, three young outsiders from Washington, DC, one of whom was my father, Ed Snider, had taken Philly by storm as the new face of the Philadelphia Eagles, riding on the shoulders of real-estate rock star Jerry Wolman, who became the NFL's youngest owner at 36. And Lou Scheinfeld, covering City Hall for the *Philadelphia Daily News*, hit it off with the brash upstarts. A few short years later, my dad hired him to help launch both the Philadelphia Flyers and the Spectrum, which Lou named. And that was just the beginning of a half-century saga of business and friendship.

For 20 years, Scheinfeld was Snider's top gun. As Lou says in the book, "Ed knew business, I knew Philly." Few people today could imagine how important Lou's role was in those early years. His personality, wit and guile were just what Ed Snider needed when he needed help the most. The NHL didn't want Ed. The City didn't believe him. And nobody had ever attended a rock concert.

When hockey fans think of the Flyers, they think of Bobby Clarke—his gap-toothed grin on one side of the Stanley Cup, with Bernie Parent on the other. But on the inside, behind the scenes, I will always remember Lou Scheinfeld as the Bobby Clarke of the organization, the guy Ed Snider relied on in the best and worst of times. And he always got it done. From the madcap day in Montreal in June 1967 when Lou sprinted across a divided highway just in time to deliver the Flyers' franchise fee to a dour Clarence Campbell, to Kate Smith's appearance the day the Flyers won the cup.

Scheinfeld is one of the last cowboys standing from the Wild West of league expansions, the birth of the modern indoor arena and the rock 'n roll shows that followed. Lou is not your average corporate type, and that's a good thing because there was no playbook. But even if there were, he wouldn't have followed it. And if he had, the Flyers and Spectrum would not have been the same.

Lou is an original thinker, a street-smart creative with few equals. During his heyday, every day and every event was different. He was a kid in a candy shop. In this memoir, he shares the most unforgettable moments of a life lived behind the scenes in which the city came together as one and forged a new winning identity.

At big events, everybody wants something: the stars, the fans, the politicians, the press. As a younger man, I never knew why Lou stood behind the back row of the suite at every Flyers game even though he had a seat. A thousand things go on and Lou had a beat on all of it. This book tells not just what happened but thankfully what didn't happen on Lou's watch.

Looking back at the photographs and stories in this memoir, I am only beginning to fully appreciate just what these young bucks pulled off. The Flyers and the Spectrum each became the envy of other cities around the country and the world. That Lou Scheinfeld was there every step of the way is not a coincidence.

Lou is more than a friend—he's family. And I wonder where one of my wild-eyed dreams might have gone with a man like him by my side. In an age where sports teams are owned by corporations or billionaires who made their fortune elsewhere, young people will be inspired by this crazy tale, a master class in the art of what is possible.

Craig Snider

(Eldest son of Ed Snider)

1

Glory Daze Gone

The Spectrum Is a Wreck

It comes in like a wrecking ball. Never hits so hard.

Four massive tons of concrete violating the gracious wall of native red brick.

Brute force against an *object d'amour* that deserved better.

The Spectrum doesn't wince, merely puffs red dust, as though the grand old dame's enjoying one last smoke. Bruce Springsteen's "Wrecking Ball" blasts over the speakers as the hundreds of silent fans gathered under this miserable November sky say goodbye to "America's Showplace."

Finally, after a half-dozen thudding whacks, the outer layer of brick crumbles, exposing gray cinderblock. More painful hits follow, ripping an ungainly hole in the soul of this 43-year-old arena.

Atop the temporary stage in the parking lot, misty and morose, I stare at the sad spectacle along with an emotional Ed Snider, Hall of Famers Julius Erving of the 76ers, the Flyers' Bobby Clarke and Bernie Parent.

An execution in slow motion.

How can this be happening? Why wasn't this famous structure—which had thrilled generations at basketball, hockey, concerts, circus, boxing, wrestling and ice shows—saved?

I thought I had found a new life for it—a combination sports museum, brew pub and TV/movie studio—but Ed Snider's brass, ensconced in their plush offices less than a football field across the lot, pretty much wanted it gone: less bother and more parking revenue.

Sure, that glitzy new spaceship, the Wells Fargo Center, now housed all the big events, with its Vegas-worthy video board, scads of luxury suites, expensive restaurants and elaborate team shops.

But wasn't there a use for this venerable, 19,000-seat venue where the sound was so great that every major act still wanted to appear? And weren't the seats so close to the action that you could hear the grunts and smell the sweat?

Hadn't the Flyers' cult-crazy Broad Street Bullies won both of their Stanley Cups there and dominated for so many years? And isn't it where the 76ers had some of their most memorable battles against the hated Boston Celtics and swept the LA Lakers en route to the 1983 NBA championship?

It's where Dr. J soared, Sir Charles roared and Clarkie scored. Let's not forget the famous shot in the greatest college game ever, where Christian Laettner's impossible buzzer-beater stunned Kentucky and propelled Duke to the 1982 NCAA Finals. Then there was Kate Smith and the Flyers' magical "God Bless America" legend, which many years later ended on a sad note as it came to light that a few songs she sang as a young woman were considered racist by today's standards.

How about the Russian game where the brutalized Soviet Red Army team walked off the ice in 1976, only to return after Flyers owner Snider dashed from his box to the locker room and threatened to withhold payment for the Russkies' North American tour?

Flyers announcer Gene Hart, who spoke Russian, interpreted as Snider told the team manager to get his squad back on the ice. The manager refused, claiming, "You make damage on my players." Snider asked tour boss Alan Eagleson whether the Soviets had yet been paid for the four-game NHL trip, in which the Soviets already had beaten the NY Rangers 7–3, tied the Montreal Canadiens 3–3, and defeated the Boston Bruins 5–3.

Remember, this was the height of the Cold War, feelings were raw and most of the Free World, including Flyers' haters world-wide, were rooting for the Bullies to save the day.

Eagleson said they hadn't received any money yet and a pissed Snider snapped, "Tell him that if they don't finish the game, they're not getting paid." The Russians promptly returned to the ice where the Flyers continued to hammer them, winning 4–1.

And wasn't this the building where banners hanging from the rafters boasted of sellouts for, among others, the Grateful Dead (53), Bruce Springsteen (42) and Billy Joel (25)?

Only a few weeks before the wrecking ball, the old building closed with a different kind of bang. Both Springsteen and Pearl Jam's Eddie Vedder wanted to be the last band standing.

Courteously, Bruce's camp agreed to let Pearl Jam turn off the lights. Each band then played for four consecutive nights, serving up an eight-gig salute worthy of the big hall.

Springsteen, who had been booed off the building's stage in 1973 when he opened for the band Chicago, took his last appearance there to shout out to the audience, "The Spectrum will live forever! They don't make buildings like this anymore."

But that was a long time ago and far away. Running the Spectrum and the Flyers organizations in the belly of the beast of an arena back then was a whole different animal. The staffs were small and like family. There were only nine of us in the Flyers office; the 76ers had even fewer.

There were no computers, cell phones, fax machines, focus groups or anything called sports marketing. Analytics? What the hell is that?

Carbon paper and piles of pink phone message slips. Remington typewriters and A. B. Dick mimeograph machines. Secretaries took dictation on steno pads and everyone carried a pocketful of dimes to stay in touch via ubiquitous pay telephones.

Basketball and hockey players had part-time jobs to support themselves. Boxers and wrestlers kept up their day jobs. Spectrum favorites Bennie Briscoe, the rock-solid middleweight boxer, was a city trash collector. George "The Animal" Steele was a New Jersey schoolteacher named William James Myers.

It was a different time, before big arena concerts, with only selected sports coverage on radio and small black-and-white TVs.

The 1960s and the early '70s were also scary times with Jack and Bobby Kennedy as well as Martin Luther King, Jr. assassinated, seething protests over Vietnam carnage and racial riots roiling the nation. A worn LBJ gave way to Tricky Dick Nixon, and you know how that went.

Philly was a crappy, scrappy town back then with only two or three decent restaurants. The most famous, Old Original Bookbinder's, was a tourist trap where locals splurged only for special occasions, unless you knew Johnny Taxin, its stout, garrulous owner. Then, you personally were ushered into a clubby booth in the front bar reserved for celebs such as the Franks—Rizzo, Sinatra, and Palumbo—Grace Kelly, Leonard Tose, Steve Carlton, Dick Clark, Wilt Chamberlain, auto dealer Victor Potamkin, "Smokin'" Joe Frazier and, of course, natty mobsters.

The Philly Mafia was a docile one in the sixties under Angelo "the Gentle Don" Bruno, who didn't brook drug traffic or violence, but tightly controlled the region's cigarette and other vending machine business—and maybe a few mini slot machines tucked away in corner stores and bars.

Hippies, mini-skirts and discos were in—and bras were out. Free love was a joy. Panty hose was brand new, but ladies still wore sexy garter belts holding thigh-high, lace-topped stockings, and guys looked cool in pegged pants, wide collar shirts and bell bottoms. It was tough to resist the siren call of the times.

I tooled around in a used, dark blue '65 Pontiac Bonneville convertible with a Pep Boys knob affixed to the steering wheel for cool turning. Rich people drove big Lincolns and Cadillacs —and if you saw a couple of Mercedes a year, it was a lot. BMW? What's that?

I would spend the next half-century known as "Snider's Guy," a sometime best friend, confidant and quite often, his conscience. It was like a marriage: devotion, fulfillment, reward, betrayal, anger, divorce and—after many years—an unlikely reconciliation.

But that's a story for another day.

Right now, at the demolition, I'm harking back to September 30, 1967, the very first night we opened, with the two-day Quaker City Jazz Festival. Parking was a buck, hot dogs, 35 cents and a large Coke, two bits.

Watching the wrecking ball inflict cruel and unusual punishment took me back even further, to that winter day in late 1966 when, as vice president of the fledgling arena project, I donned a construction helmet and mud boots and plodded through the unfinished building, desperate to come up with a memorable name for it.

Our biz cards and letterheads were calling it "The New Sports Arena" as a placeholder. I knew the permanent title had to be something special, something grand, something colorful and unique. I didn't want the word "arena" anywhere near it, nor a dead politician or anything to do with any war. However, one of our executives, a nice guy but not exactly a creative genius, had a pet name and was determined to make it stick.

He wanted it named "Keystone Arena."

Pennsylvania, students of the arcane might recall, is known as the Keystone State, since it sat in the very middle of the country's thirteen original colonies. A keystone is a wedge-shaped piece at the crown of an arch that locks the other pieces in place, a stone on which the other pieces depend for support. Politically, Pennsylvania played a vital role in holding together the states of the newly formed union.

With the construction clock ticking, I walked up, over and around the bare structure with our rep, Bill Becker, from Mel Richman, Inc., one of the nation's top design firms, which boasted blue-ribbon clients including Campbell's Soup, Coca-Cola and Omega watches.

I was a cocky 30-year-old who had made my mark as a hot-shot reporter and editor for the *Philadelphia Daily News*, when newspapers held great power and influence.

Now, as vice president in charge of making the arena and hockey team first class, I was determined that it be named something short and punchy—with strength and color.

So, side-stepping scores of McCloskey Construction Company's iron workers, pipefitters and carpenters and dodging fearsome cranes ferrying heavy loads to the second deck, we started throwing out names: *Super . . . Superb . . . Supercalifragilistic . . . Spectacular . . . Splendid . . . Splendiforous . . . Special . . . Stadia . . . Specter . . . Spectrum.* Hmm, *Spectrum.* Hmm, again.

Bill swore he uttered it first and maybe he did. I honestly don't remember.

I wasn't sure exactly what it meant, but said if it's anything close to what I envisioned, "We're going with it."

Rushing back to my "New Sports Arena" and "Hockey Club" offices at 15th and Locust Streets in center city, I made a beeline for the big Webster's dictionary that sat open on a wooden rolling cart, standard in most schools and offices at the time. I found *spectrum* to mean, among other things, a band of colors as seen in a rainbow, colors emanating from a prism, everything colorful under the sun, images which form displays.

That's us, I thought. That's what we're presenting—everything colorful under the sun.

"Holy shit!" I shouted.

Secretaries looked up from their typewriters, a hockey scout gave me the Canadian "eh?" and an annoyed accountant, who didn't realize history was about to be made, shook his head and went back to his bore-ass ledger book.

"We're gonna name it the Spectrum," I yelled. "The God damn Spectrum!"

"The what?" someone said.

"Huh?"

"What's a spectrum?"

I had to move the organization away from the deadly "Keystone Arena" moniker, so I quickly scheduled a presentation with decision-makers, including owner Jerry Wolman.

I told Becker to have Mel Richman designers bang out a knock-your-socks-off, big board presentation with a splashy "Spectrum" logo. Then I stopped at an old gas station on Broad St. and "borrowed" a rusty, metal Keystone Inspection Station sign sitting next to an unwatched side bay.

Back at the office, I grabbed the Yellow Pages phone book, scribbled some notes and was all set.

The presentation was to take place in Snider's big corner office in the Philadelphia Eagles' flashy headquarters on the ground floor of the *Evening Bulletin* newspaper building at 30th and Market Streets, across from stately 30th Street Station.

Snider was executive vice-president of the Birds and, in addition to running the football team, was overseeing construction of the arena and formation of the new hockey team. Wolman, a successful Washington, DC mega-developer and owner of the Eagles, shared Snider's office at the large conference table when he was in town a couple times a month.

The Eagles had set up the hockey team and arena as separate entities after convincing the National Hockey League in February 1966 to award one of its six expansion franchises to Philly. Wolman gave Snider a considerable chunk of the building and of the team, on top of the 7-percent piece of the Eagles he already held. Wolman routinely gave aides pieces of ownership to cement their loyalty while he pursued his developer's dreams.

I was scheduled to present at 2:00 p.m., but it wasn't until nearly 4 o'clock, long after lunch but not yet happy hour, when the intercom buzzed on the desk of Snider's pretty brunette secretary, Maryanne, who told me they were ready.

"Showtime," I said to myself, pushing open the thick glass door to the executive office.

Seated around the polished mahogany conference table, in addition to Wolman and Snider, were hockey team president Bill Putnam, a former Morgan Guaranty Trust banker, who had put the deal together to win the NHL franchise; Joe King, Eagles business manager; arena president Hal "Mr. Keystone Arena" Freeman, newly promoted to the project from his Eagles public relations position; Jerry Schiff, Snider's affable brother-in-law, who headed a small construction firm; Eagles much-maligned head coach Joe Kuharich; Eagles PR director Bill Heffernan, a respected former *Bulletin* sports reporter; arena architect Phillip Zielinsky from Chicago's prestigious Skidmore, Owings and Merrill, Inc.; and sharp-as-a-tack Eagles attorney Earl Foreman, who was married to Snider's older sister, Phyllis.

Ties were undone, sleeves rolled up and those still wearing suit jackets looked weary from another marathon meeting with Wolman in town. The table was covered with blueprints, half-empty china coffee cups, stub-filled ash trays, financial statements and contracts — the corporate detritus of a big-time business session.

Not exactly the Nuremberg Jury, but certainly not thrilled to see me at this time of day, especially my boss, Mr. Freeman. (Ironically, five years later I would watch him leave the Spectrum with his belongings in a cardboard box as I replaced him as president of the arena.)

I knew I had to get with it and weighed in immediately, setting my show-and-tell boards on an easel Maryanne had ordered for me.

"Gentlemen," I said brightly, "we have an opportunity to make history. We're going to name our state-of-the-art entertainment center something so spectacular that people all over the country are going to sit up and go 'Wow!'"

"We're going to call it 'The Spectrum.'"

Silence.

Deafening silence!

"The what?"

But I saw the architect and Earl Foreman smile, which was a good sign.

I continued with my spiel, displaying the first poster board containing a slick Spectrum logo in four colors. Then, a second board showing the Spectrum name emblazoned over the entrance of a rendition of the building. A third showed a cute usherette and a handsome security guy in uniform, replete with jacket and hat Spectrum patches.

The last boards showed a full-page, national color advertisement for magazines and a black-and-white one for newspapers.

I had a few more boards but decided less was more and launched into the meaning of the word: "Images which form displays . . . colors emanating from a prism . . . everything colorful under the sun . . . colors of a rainbow."

I had everyone's full attention by now and was pumped.

"And, by the way, there is no company in Pennsylvania, New Jersey or Delaware named 'Spectrum.'

"However," I said quite seriously, "there is another name that has been proposed . . . 'Keystone Arena.'"

"A worthy name. In fact, so popular that there are already 63 companies in the area named 'Keystone,' including the Keystone Nuts & Bolts Company, Keystone Pickle Works, Keystone Tonsorial Parlor (next to the Troc burlesque house on Arch Street), and last but not least, the ever-popular Keystone Massage Parlor, discreetly located under the Walt Whitman Bridge."

Then I produced the—uh—appropriated inspection station sign shaped like a keystone and said, "We don't even have to design a logo."

Heavy handed? Yes. Overkill? Of course. But as a tough city detective once told me, "You wanna win a street fight, soon as the guy puts up his dukes, kick him in the balls." Fight over!

Hal then said a few words on behalf of "Keystone Arena." Wolman said we need to pick a name now, and asked me to step out of the room.

About 15 minutes later, Snider buzzed Maryanne with a message that I should meet him later at Lou Mayo's Bellevue Court restaurant, one of our favorite watering holes, tucked behind the Bellevue Stratford Hotel.

I was nursing my second V.O. on the rocks with a lemon peel when Snider finally arrived about 7:00 p.m., wearing a serious look.

"We voted," he said. "It was nine to one."

"For?"

"Spectrum," he said grinning.

YES!

"But . . ."

Shit! The dreaded "but."

"Hal said the vote should be put to the entire Eagles staff."

Oh, crap!

Nice guy Hal was very popular among Eagles' office workers. I liked him too, but we had different ideas on how to run things. I had wild ideas. He played it tame. I liked to make waves. He didn't want to rock the boat.

As an example, one day weeks earlier, Ed Snider had come by the 15th Street offices to say he was disappointed with my contributions to the project so far and wasn't seeing the ballsy effort he expected when he hired me away from the *Daily News*.

"I thought you would've shown a lot more positive force by now," he said. "Where are all those great ideas you talked about?"

"Bottom left drawer, Hal's desk," I replied.

"Huh?"

I explained that most every project I proposed, in detailed memos, went into that drawer to die.

Snider stood immediately and headed down the hall to Hal's office. After some small talk, he related later, he asked Hal how I had been doing, saying I told him I had given Hal a bunch of ideas, but none had materialized.

Hal reached down, opened his drawer and removed about a dozen neatly folded memos that he told Ed were too risky or unproven to pursue.

Snider said he looked them over, told Hal he thought most were good if not great ideas and the kind of forward thinking he expected for the project. Ed then told me to copy him on all future proposals.

From that day, Hal reluctantly gave me the green light to move on most of my proposals, but he clearly was not a happy camper and our relationship chilled.

The Eagles' staff Spectrum–Keystone vote was held the next day. Hal pitched his colleagues. I wasn't invited, but my boards were displayed—minus my brilliant, smart-assed commentary.

Ed called me after the vote. The final tally . . . 30–1.

Ouch!

And thus was born "The Spectrum."

I felt for Hal, but like my hero Popeye sez: "I yam what I yam!"

2

The Candy Store
Dad's Shop to the Big Top

So here I am at my big-ass marble Knoll desk in the bowels of the Spectrum eating not a bowl of South Philly pasta, but a bucket of shit from one of the town's mobsters.

"Don't worry," I try to mansplain to Dominic, "I already straightened it out!"

"Straighten this out, you dumb shit!" he yells into the phone and hangs up on me. But not before sweetly adding, "and go fuckaya mother!"

This is no small matter.

The Chairman, Frank Sinatra, is playing the Spectrum for two sold-out-to-the-rafters shows in three weeks, and if I don't make things right, Ol' Blue Eyes is gonna dump Philly and instead do one big gig in Atlantic City's cavernous Convention Hall 60 miles away.

This unfortunate turn, of course, could get me not only fired from my dream job as president of the arena, but dumped into that monstrous car crusher in South Philly, a section of the city where legions of paisanos worship Frankie Boy.

None of this is my fault, of course, but if the Crooner is pissed—that makes it my problem.

What happened was a fuck-up of epic proportions involving a switcheroo on a stack of tickets, threats to my well-being and a notorious goon sitting at my desk brandishing a snub-nosed .38.

I already took care of this mix-up in a block of tickets Sinatra wanted reserved for the Philly Teamsters, but apparently word didn't get to the local boys. There's lots more on this in Chapter 10 about the Philly Mob muscling me.

■ ■ ■

Anyway, running a big-city arena with basketball giants, toothless hockey toughs and concert heavyweights like Frank, Elvis, Barbra, Jagger, Liberace, Daltrey and Judy Garland is no small task. Mix in characters involved in boxing, wrestling, circus, ice shows, college hoops and truck pulls, and you got yourself one big candy store—on steroids.

But let me start at the beginning, about me.

The Candy Store.

I had a great childhood. When I recount my stories today or just think back, they replay like a black-and-white episode in the early, awesome days of television. My memories are also a magic quilt, stitched and sewn from fragments of a much simpler time.

I came into this world after the worst of the Great Depression and before World War II. It was November 25, 1935, three days before Thanksgiving, and with President Franklin D. Roosevelt in the White House, there was relief that while war and strife occurred far away, America, at least, was at peace.

We lived in a three-story row house behind and over the candy store that my parents, Alexander and Frances, operated for 51 years at 30th Street and Girard Avenue in the very blue-collar Brewerytown section of Philadelphia. Al's Variety Store, four blocks from the nation's oldest zoo and twenty blocks from center city, was a beehive of all kinds of action. Once there were six big breweries operating within blocks. As kids, we played in their deserted carcasses, running through the subterranean brick caves that were built to cool barrels of brew before refrigeration.

People came in and out of our popular store from 6:30 a.m. until closing at 11:30 p.m. Neighbors, workers off PTC's Number 15 trolley and strollers heading to nearby Fairmount Park for spring water or picnics stopped in to buy something, or just to kibitz.

We were the hub of the neighborhood, where hundreds of families counted on us to be open seven days a week so they could buy everyday items such as cigarettes and cigars, ice cream, newspapers, magazines, film, over-the-counter medicines, hosiery and school supplies. Money was tight but life was good, and I loved being in the middle of all the action, just like I would years later in running my arena.

Girard Avenue was very different back then. Everyone knew everyone, families were close, and neighbors looked out for one another.

Today, it's a gentrified mix of old-timers on pensions and millennials on iPads. Inhabited then by mostly Germans and Irish, we were one of the few Jewish families. We also were one of the only stores around with telephone service. It was my job, at ten years old, with wispy hair and wild energy, to "run calls."

When a phone rang in one of our two classic Bell Telephone booths in the rear of the small store, my mother would answer "Al's," ask the caller to hold and yell, "Louis! Run around the corner and tell Mrs. Mink she's wanted on the phone!"

So, run around the corner to Mrs. Mink's I did, fast as I could, up 30th and over tiny Flora Street to her little row house with the worn brownstone steps that sat smack next to the cramped Frank's Beverages soda plant housed in an old garage.

I delivered my message as if I were a soldier on the front lines, then flew back to breathlessly tell whoever was calling that "Mrs. Mink is on her way!" Paul Revere was no bigger hero.

Who knew that 20 years later I would make a mad dash across Dorchester Street, a busy boulevard in Montreal, and up the steps of the regal Queen Elizabeth Hotel, clutching the two-million-dollar check that secured the Flyers hockey franchise for Philadelphia? We almost missed the deadline and Baltimore would have gotten the NHL expansion franchise instead. But that's a yarn for a chapter coming up.

As Mrs. Mink yakked with God knows who, I would loiter nearby, because when she was done, that little old lady with white hair and overly rouged cheeks would hand me a nickel. Mrs. Mink got a lot of calls. One lucrative summer, between the gabby Mrs. Mink, the crazy Olson family and the big and scary "Reverend" Callahan, among others, I made almost four dollars! I also got a nickel allowance every Saturday and was allowed to keep any coins I was brave enough to recover that rolled under our old marble soda fountain into a dark and fusty no-man's land.

The imposing Reverend had established a church of dubious distinction in a row house down the street. Dressed head to toe in black, with a commanding silver belt buckle preceding his girth like a Packard hood ornament, he scared the shit out of me.

I think the only other person who ever made me feel so diminished was many years later when I encountered a naked, dripping Wilt Chamberlain exiting the shower in a Spectrum locker room. Imagine Wilt, at 7'1" and nearly 300 pounds, looming over me as I'm down on one knee lacing up a sneaker for a workout.

Try to unsee that picture.

Into the store the Reverend came most every afternoon for his "Bromo." My dad or I concocted this bubbly mix by turning a knob that plopped white powder into a paper cup from a large bottle of Bromo Seltzer that was inverted on a metal stand. Then we'd blast it with a needle stream of carbonated water from our fountain faucet. He would chug it, buy a bottle of the powdered stuff and go. A nickel for the fizzy drink, twelve cents for a bottle.

After about a year, this scary giant was found dead in his "house of worship" among scores of empty Bromo bottles. Truly, the Bromo King! I later heard he had been a prison guard at nearby Eastern State Penitentiary and got fired after legendary bank robber Willie Sutton tunneled his way out in 1947 and escaped.

Every day after school at 4 o'clock, it was time to listen to the serials of my radio heroes. As I lay on the floor of our little living room behind the store, staring at the ceiling, The Lone Ranger galloped across the rug and Sky King zoomed overhead in his awesome plane, Songbird, capturing spies and rescuing lost hikers on a deserted Arizona trail. I had no idea where Arizona was—just that it was way past West Philly.

While my mother prepared dinner in the shed of a kitchen two steps up from the living room, my sister Suzanne would join me around our old Philco cathedral radio, as it brought to life *Jack Armstrong, the All-American Boy, Don Winslow of the Navy, Captain Midnight* and *Flash Gordon*. The shows were 30 minutes long with tons of enticing commercials sponsored by Kellogg's cereals, Ovaltine® chocolate-malt drink, and General Food's Post Toasties®.

Secret decoders, decals, rings and other magical items were available by mailing in box tops and product labels with a nickel or dime taped to a piece of cardboard. We would stuff the material in envelopes, add the penny postage stamp and wait for six to eight weeks (or forever) for the prize to arrive.

Listening to these shows, my mind ran wild, and I pictured myself as every hero imaginable, saving people, countries, even galaxies! I already knew I wanted to do big things, which didn't include spending my life behind a candy store counter, as had done my father and his father before.

After the shows, Suzanne, who was almost five years older than I, would do her homework, while I would watch Dad tend store and dip ice cream for cones and make frothy fountain sodas with seltzer water and hand-pumped syrups. Eventually, I was helping him. After years of dipping and scraping frozen mounds of ice cream, my right forearm grew much bigger than my left. Whenever I saw cartoon moments of Popeye downing his can of spinach and kayoing Brutus with his tattooed weapon of an arm, it made me feel better about my lack of biceps symmetry.

Our neighbors depended on our store not only for phone calls, candy and sodas, but for things like over-the-counter medicines, newspapers and smokes. At only a dozen feet wide and maybe three times that long, every inch at Al's was crammed with all kinds of goods.

My mom, born Frances Chiger, was a short round woman with a large bosom and an even bigger heart. She had a warm smile and a calm demeanor and was the best piano player I had ever heard. My teachers at John Sartain School, five blocks away at 30th and Oxford Streets, told me quite seriously that the only reason I graduated from eighth grade was that my mom was the school's piano player.

In the evenings, while my Dad would take a break to listen to the Milton Berle, Red Skelton or *Lux Radio Theater* shows on the living room radio, Mom and I would take over. She would don her apron and start stocking the shelves and I would take my usual position behind the counter, dipping ice cream for people who came by for a taste of Breyers heaven. Neighbors would bring bowls of all sizes for any-where from four to a dozen hand dips of various flavors.

Others ate ice cream or sundaes at the counter from pointy paper cup inserts in shiny metal holders, or they sipped milkshakes, ice cream sodas or fountain sodas. From fountain syrup dispensers we made orange, root beer, cherry, lemon, vanilla, chocolate or Coca-Cola sodas. Sundaes would be topped with gooey caramel or chocolate syr-ups and spooned marshmallow, wet walnuts, crushed cherries or pineapples. Facing the counter were four fixed, cast iron stools cov-ered in white porcelain that could spin like tops. Across from the counter was a wall of magazines, comic books and a Hallmark greet-ing card cabinet.

When I was 12, I had my first real summer job helping Hymie, the *Daily News* driver, distribute his papers. Every morning around 10:00 when he dropped off a dozen copies of the Two Star Edition at our store, I'd hop in his truck and spend the next two hours zigzagging through North Philly on his route. I sat on an old wooden soda crate behind Hymie. Safety belts? Hell, there weren't even doors!

When he'd pull up in front of a candy store or grocery, I'd grab whatever number of the tabloids he'd holler, leap from the truck and go in yelling "Daily News!" I'd stick the papers in a rack or on a bench, grab yesterday's returns and hustle back to the truck. I loved this job.

It was a hot summer and the breeze felt great. Plus I got to see all the other mom and pop corner stores in the nearby Fairmount and Strawberry Mansion sections. Hymie would flip me a quarter when he dropped me back home. What could be better? (Actually, better was when I later worked for the *Daily News* as a reporter covering City Hall and hobnobbed with mayors, governors and the city's movers and shakers.)

By the time I was 15, all that Breyers dipping gave me one of the strongest right arms in the neighborhood. As one of the few Jewish kids in Brewerytown, my sister and I often were the target of "the Goyim"—the tough gentile kids who thought it was fun to play "get the Jew." But like Popeye versus Brutus, I became a force to be reckoned with.

A few days after a brief street fight where I nearly broke another kid's jaw, I was challenged by one of the neighborhood's older toughs. He offered to arm-wrestle—a big mistake! I wore him down, pinned him and poured it on until he literally cried "uncle." I was sending a message. After that, most kids left me and my sister alone.

The prowess of my right arm became sort of a thing in my neighborhood. I would excitedly arm-wrestle grown men—welders from Budd's auto chassis plant, Greyhound bus drivers, Schmidt's Beer brewers—and either hold them to a draw or pin them. Losing was unthinkable. I would hang on until my arm fell off. My righty was a Brutus-beating beast!

Despite my weapon-grade arm, I was extremely shy around adults, girls and high school classmates from better neighborhoods. While many of my friends at the elite Central High were getting laid, I had yet to get to "second base."

When I was 21 and in my junior year in Temple University's School of Journalism, I started dating an equally inexperienced girl. She was sweet and innocent; I was young and horny. One thing led to another and we had to get married, so we eloped to Elkton, Maryland, about an hour south of Philadelphia.

Our marriage lasted nearly 20 years while producing four great kids. But we eventually found ourselves on divergent paths. She remained shy and demure while I was into the heady action as a reporter and eventually the faster pace at the Spectrum.

My first job out of Temple in 1957 forced me to confront my shyness in dramatic fashion. I landed an entry-level job writing mostly obituaries and small news pieces for the *Trentonian*. After several weeks, I was sent to cover the impaneling of a jury at the Trenton Courthouse but found myself blocked at the courtroom door.

A knot of cops, lawyers and assorted court gadflies were jammed there, but when I heard the bailiff call things to order, I realized this was my moment of truth. "Louis, time to shit or get off the pot," as my mother would say.

Taking a deep breath and channeling every reporter from every newspaper movie I had ever seen, I yelled, "PRESS!" and launched my 6-foot, 185-pound frame into the throng.

Like a fullback bursting through the line and into the clear, I was immediately greeted by court officers who dutifully hustled me to the press table right up front. They handed me sheets of information, brought me water and catered to my every need with names, dates and details.

So this is how it works. The power of the press. Awesome!

I grew a pair that day. After that, dealing with pols, celebs and powerful leaders was a snap. I was 23, hard as a rock, and ready to roll.

Back to my childhood: Life in the store, in school and with my growing love of sports was just fine because I was strong and smart and confident.

While growing up, almost every night after we closed the store, I enjoyed a black-and-white milk shake, a perfect concoction of just the right blend of chocolate syrup, milk and Breyers vanilla ice cream, whirred on that marvelous, green Hamilton Beach mixer. I would partner that with either a package of Lance Toast Chee® crackers or a Tastykake Chocolate Junior®. Mom would smooth out the waxed Tastykake wrapper, put it in the drawer with dozens of others and re-use it to wrap our lunches. My mom, the Waxed Wrapper Queen.

I still have that beloved 1940s Hamilton shaker and use it often. Still whirrs up delicious black-and-whites. None of that soft Dairy Queen goop or yuppie Häagen-Dazs around my house. It's Breyers or bust.

Every Sunday at 1:00 p.m. sharp, we would close the store and stick the little cardboard clock card in the window. The red tin hands were set to the back-at-seven position. Our family then had six glorious hours before we reopened to dip mounds of ice cream and provide notions that people needed for Monday work or school.

Things like Kodak film no. 120 for their Brownies; unfiltered cigarettes named Old Gold, Philip Morris, Chesterfield, Raleigh, Fatima, Marvel, Wings, Camels and Lucky Strike; cigars named Royalist, Dutch Master, Phillies five-cent cigars, and White Owl "three for a quarter" stogies; Copenhagen snuff; Kotex and Modess sanitary napkins in big, clunky boxes; Arrid deodorant; Toni ("Which Twin Has the Toni") hair treatment; Shinola liquid shoe polish with its lid-attached, brush applicator; Phillips' Milk of Magnesia; needle and thread; bobby pins, hair nets and hot water bottles; bottles of Coke, Pepsi, Frank's, Booth's, Hires and Dad's Old Fashioned Root Beer; Anacin for headaches and Doan's Little Liver Pills; newspapers including the *Inquirer, Daily News, Public Ledger, Bulletin* and *Record*; magazines called *Life, Look, Colliers, Argosy, Police Gazette, Hollywood Confidential, Saturday Evening Post* and *Sport*.

We had just about everything within our reach, stacked on the narrow shelves on the wall behind the counter: Stuff to treat toothaches, menstruation, diarrhea or constipation, insomnia, stomach ills, depression, and the need for sex: condoms—then called "prophylactics" or "rubbers" or "safes"—and whatever else ailed our customers. We even had something called Dr. Young's rectal dilators. What they were for, I still don't want to know.

On Sunday afternoons after closing, we quickly showered, dressed up and walked downtown to catch a matinee at one of the grand cinema houses along Market Street with names like the Fox, Earl, Stanley, Mastbaum (with more than 4,700 seats), Boyd, Aldine, Stanton, Arcadia and Trans-Lux. One theater, appropriately named the News, showed nothing but newsreels. Another movie house, whose name I can't recall, showed only cartoons, so we never went there. Some of these palaces also presented elaborate stage shows and legitimate theater, but not on Sundays, as prohibited by Philly's Quaker-inspired Blue Laws. Eclectic architectural styles such as Spanish, North African and Art-Deco lit up theaters in center city and in nearly every neighborhood across the city. We had the Fairmount movie theater only four blocks down Girard Avenue, where we'd collect a set of free dishes or silverware by attending on consecutive Monday nights.

Amid the Sunday bustle of center city, we'd usually grab dinner at the Horn & Hardart's automat on Market Street or at Kelly's Seafood on Twelfth, across from the Reading Terminal. After dinner we'd either hoof it back home or take the No. 9 trolley for a 7-1/2-cent token each. We didn't have a car and a cab was out of the question.

Of the two things that changed me as a kid, the first was at one of our weekly Sunday dinners out, and the other was at the old Arena in West Philly. One Sunday when I was 13 or 14, something happened that set a course in stone for the rest of my life. On our way home, we came upon a pretty, young lady about 19 or 20 waiting alone for the No. 15 trolley at 29th and Girard in front of the corner taproom. It was Easter Sunday and she was wearing a white bonnet, a blue dress with a wide, white belt and white heels.

A sloppy, red-faced drunk was bothering her. "C'mon, give me a little kissh," he slurred. She was scared, on the verge of tears and was backing away from him.

"Get away . . . Leave me alone."

I thought for sure my father, like the Lone Ranger in his white hat, would come to her rescue and chase him off.

Instinctively, I started toward the drunk, but Dad grabbed my arm and ushered us past the ugly scene. The girl looked at us pleadingly, but we just continued walking. I was so ashamed. I never forgot it.

My dad fell off the pedestal that day. We never discussed it, but as I got older, I came to understand he was protecting us. It took me a long time to finally forgive him, but that came with having children of my own whom I never would put in harm's way. To this day it haunts me, wondering what happened to the scared girl in the white bonnet. I can't tell you how many times I've killed that drunken bastard in my head.

I made up my mind that I would never do what my father had done. I lost a hero that day—and vowed to become one. Because of that, I've interceded more than a few times when someone needed help. Sometimes it worked out, sometimes it didn't. A couple of times I got slugged and bear the scars to prove it.

One night, a guy flashed a gun on me when I jumped in to stop him from beating a man who was already on the ground. My first wife, Myra, and I were driving from Atlantic City to our beach house in Ventnor one sticky July night after dinner. We had enjoyed a great meal at one of our favorite spots, the Knife & Fork Inn, and were in a great mood. Heading up Ventnor Avenue, I saw what looked like a very unfair fight. The guy on the ground was getting the crap beat out of him. I slammed on the brakes, flew out of the car and spun the attacker around. "Back the fuck off," he snarled. "I'm a cop!"

Bent over with his right hand holding the guy down by the neck, he lifted his jacket with his left. On his belt I saw a gold badge and the black handle of a revolver.

"Oh, shit!" I realized. "He's a detective."

With nowhere to go, however, I came on strong.

"I don't care who you are, you don't beat a guy who's on the ground."

The cop placed his hand on his gun butt and started facing me down.

"You don't know who you're messing with, asshole," he said.

I was getting anxious about how this would play out when I noticed a half-dozen people witnessing the scene. Just as the cop let go of the guy, took out his cuffs and took a step toward me, the people started chanting: "Police brutality!... Police brutality!"

Standoff. Thank God!

As if on cue, a squad car pulled up and two patrolmen got out. Sizing up the situation, they hustled the drunken sap into the car. He was bruised, but not badly hurt.

The detective eyed the growing crowd, shot me a nasty look and backed off. "Don't ever let me see you around, you fuck," he spat, ducking into the police car next to the drunk as off it sped. The crowd applauded, and I took a bow and a quick exit.

My wife, who watched the whole stupid scene from the car, still in the middle of the street, driver's door open and engine running, was shook and angry—and not necessarily in that order.

"Are you crazy?" she said. "You could've gotten yourself arrested—or even shot!"

"Honey," I said, "you know I couldn't let that jerk beat that guy."

I would do it again and she knew it. For that scared young lady on a long-ago Easter Sunday.

The second thing that changed the course of my life was that whenever I could, I would head to 46th and Market in West Philly to sneak into another world—a fantastical magical kingdom of a building simply called "The Arena."

It wasn't exactly grand. It had only one set of entrance doors and sat in the grim shadow of the Market Street elevated train, which rattled overhead from 69th Street Terminal, under center city and back on top to the Frankford section at the other end of town, a stretch of 13 miles.

Entering those arena doors for me was like stepping out of the black-and-white farmhouse into the Technicolor® world of the Wizard of Oz. The magic that went on inside dazzled and captivated me. I wanted to live in that kingdom forever.

Louie, we're not in Philly anymore!

If I gave him a quarter, "Woz" Woznewski, the guard, would hold the fire door open for me. I would go down the back hall and around past the men's room, which reeked from stale beer and fresh urine, up the steep steps and under the stands to the arena floor. Once or twice I got unceremoniously ushered out, but I usually would find a way back in by either flashing a discarded ticket stub from another event or scrounging up 50 cents for a ticket.

The inside of the Arena was really a dump. But there were thousands of worn seats in red and gold, the colors of kings.

This was 1948, the year the National Basketball Association was formed. I watched the Philadelphia Warriors before they deserted in 1962 to San Francisco. My heroes were many. There was Villanova's "Pitchin'" Paul Arizin, one of the 50 greatest NBA players of all time, who wheezed so heavily from asthma that you thought he would never make it down the 94-foot court. Six-foot-eight Neil "The Wheel" Johnston, with his swooping hook shot and huge Adam's apple. Ernie "Boom Boom" Beck from Penn, and Jumping Joe Fulks, a dead-eye shot from Kentucky, who invented the jump shot.

I saw Kid Gavilan and Gil Turner box through the clouds of cigar smoke that pretty much obscured the view from the rafters. And my dad told me he saw the immortal Sugar Ray Robinson fight there once.

Wrestling at the Arena was another favorite pastime of mine. Antonio (Argentina) Rocca would fly through the air to deliver his devastating drop kicks, and Don Eagle, in a demonstration of pure pageantry, donned his ceremonial headdress known as his "war bonnet." The massive wrestling superstar Bruno Sammartino looked as if he came down from Mt. Olympus rather than off a bus from Pittsburgh.

There was Strangler Lewis and George "The Animal" Steele and Gorgeous George, who made Liberace look like a stud, but could knock you silly while he dispensed gold-colored hair pins to the crazed crowd.

Fans would stream to the Arena to watch the roller derby with its rawhide men and wiry women whipsawing around the banked track, slinging their teammates ahead to score points while blocking and kicking opponents over the rail and off the track. My heroes were Judy Arnold and Buddy Atkinson, Jr.

Minor league ice hockey was played there. There were the Rockets and the Arrows, who became the Ramblers. An interesting fact is that the great Philadelphia Flyers goalie Ron Hextall's grandfather was a major player for the Arrows back then. No way could I see this sport becoming a real fan favorite in Philly, like the A's or Phillies or even the Eagles. Little did I know that ice hockey would be the major player in my own life that would take me on a course that I never could have predicted.

The circus was too big to play the Arena. In those days, two circuses toured through Philly every year: Ringling Bros. and Barnum & Bailey (that was one), and the Frank "Bring 'Em Back Alive" Buck Circus played under their huge tents on a soccer field at G Street and Erie Avenue. They had elephants, clowns and lions, a trapeze and a side show that is banned today because it featured what were called "freaks," a variety of folks with grotesque birth defects, Siamese twins, the bearded fat lady and the eight-foot-tall man. Others displayed awesome talents such as sword-swallowing, fire-eating, lying on a bed of nails or walking barefoot on hot coals or broken glass. These poor souls were just trying to make the most of their talent—or misfortune.

I would take the rattling No. 15 trolley on Girard Avenue to the Broad Street subway, then to Erie Avenue, and another trolley down Erie Avenue to "Lighthouse Field" to watch in fascination when the circus trucks pulled into town every spring.

The crew, called roustabouts, would pound giant wooden stakes into the ground to anchor the thick tent ropes, and the trainers, in loud, strange languages, would cajole a squadron of elephants to strain and pull the thick ropes that miraculously raised the canvas Big Tops that the shows brought with them.

My greatest thrill back at the Arena was the day Roy Rogers and his giant horse Trigger appeared, when I was eight or nine years old. Roy would get his palomino to rear up on its hind legs and paw the air. Roy's wife, the glamorous Dale Evans, rode alongside on her horse, Buttermilk, killing off all the Indians whooping it up inside the sawdust ring. Try and pull that off today!

On this memorable day, I managed to make my way down to the front row near the end of the show, and when they rode by, I was able to reach out through the screen and touch Roy's hand and feel his magnificent sequined sleeve.

I had all his trading cards that came in the Post cereal boxes and had seen him in the movies at Saturday matinees at the Fairmount. Those were great, but this was the best! I told my dad, who brought me that day, "I'm never washing my hand again." Mom, of course, had a different idea about that when I got home.

But something tragic happened during the week that Roy Rogers played the Arena. A local girl who rode in Roy's show was thrown off her horse, broke her neck and died. She was only 20. Roy, Dale and the Sons of the Pioneers rode their horses under the El and up Market Street to the cemetery about a mile away for a ceremony where they sang "Roundup in the Sky" as part of the graveside service. I wasn't there, but I read about it in the *Evening Bulletin*.

In a way, my fabulous career got started the day I slipped my quarter to Woz for a Sunday show of the Ice Follies. He told me a soda vendor had cut himself on a broken bottle of Coke and couldn't sell. I jumped at the chance to make some dough, and with that strong right arm, I figured I could handle the heavy metal bucket of ice and bottles. Still, the sight of the bloody towel he issued to me gave me doubts.

But an older guy with tattoos on his arms and a half-cigarette behind his ear had other ideas. "I got it, kid. I got a family to feed!" He grabbed the bucket out of my hand. "There's a stack of my programs over there," he said. "Ten cents. You know how to make change? I'll talk to Woz. Just remember, kid, if you're short at the end of the night it comes out of your ass and you get to clean the head."

I had no idea what the head was until the end of the matinee, when I came up 30 cents short and wound up hosing down the urinal trough in the clammy men's room, gagging while throwing in new camphor cakes.

I continued to work there whenever I could. As the shows wore on, the steps seemed to get steeper. I didn't do very well selling programs. But I loved hawking other stuff, even the days when I didn't make much money. From programs to popcorn, hot dogs and sodas. I always faced the row at an angle so I could do my job and watch the stage at the same time. I saw comedians Bob Hope and Victor Borge, singers Nat King Cole and a young Elvis Presley. By the time Elvis came for his four shows over two days in 1957, I had worked my way up from vendor to the box office.

The Arena, with a seating capacity of about 6,000, was deteriorating, and we were losing a lot of shows to the nicer, city-owned Convention Hall about a mile away. Still, since he was already booked, Elvis performed with us. While he was on stage, some wise guys threw eggs at him. He challenged them to come down to the stage and try something.

I saw the cops haul the jerks away ("hooligans," the Daily News called 'em the next day). Many years later when Elvis played the Spectrum, I recounted that night to him. He laughed and said he remembered because it was the only time that happened to him. The King autographed his guitar strap and gave it to me. I later donated it to a charity auction, where it sold for 50 bucks.

A week or two before any of his shows at the Spectrum, Elvis's manager, Colonel Tom Parker and his crew, as was their custom, would show up to physically count every seat in the house. They'd be back the day of the event and count them again to make sure we didn't slip in any extra seats for which the King wasn't going to get paid.

The courtly Colonel, donning his usual western shirt, bolo tie and brown cowboy hat, would direct the crew by pointing his cane at each section in each tier. With a slim stogie poking out of his tan, round face, Elvis's Svengali would then match his final count to our official ticket manifest. Other buildings often would squeeze in extra seats right before the show and keep the cash, but we—wink, wink—would never do such a thing.

■ ■ ■

I reminisce about those days as I sit at my huge old desk. I witnessed magic and history as a kid, and then made it happen as an adult.

We catered to addled rockers like the Dead, Lynard Skynard, Blondie, Metallica and the Stones, and their nympho groupies, outsized egos like Barbra and Prince, bad-ass superstars Don King and Mike Tyson and their possies, 'roid-raged grapplers Hulk Hogan and a young Vince McMahon, not to mention the all-out hockey brawls on the ice—and in the stands, overdosed concert fans, box office cheats, pushy ticket brokers and demands from shady politicians, corporate assholes—and even the Mob.

I also got to hang with some great people like Dr. J., Wilt, Billy Jean King (who taught me how to serve: "Throw the ball up, swing your racquet and try to hit the scoreboard up in the ceiling. But yank your racquet down just as you hit the ball and it will drop over the net into the forecourt." It worked most every time but not nearly as efficiently for as BJK) and Bobby Clarke, Bernie Parent, Doug Collins and Billy Cunningham, Chuck Bednarik and Ron Jaworski, Joe Frazier, Kate Smith, Paul Anka, Evel Knievel, Bobby Riggs and Neil Diamond.

I'm not proud of everything I've seen or done, some of which cost me my first marriage. But I've also done a lot of good along the way, especially for people less fortunate. Like taking poor or disabled kids into the locker rooms or behind the scenes or treating disadvantaged families to shows and giving tickets and memorabilia to charities to raise money.

I've got a million stories to tell about the rock stars and sport gods, hell-raising, drugs, finance, fun, business and betrayal.

I had the greatest job in the world.

And I was damn good at it.

Let's just hope I don't fuck it up.

3

Running the Joint

Earning My Paycheck

So, what did I do as boss of an arena to earn my paycheck? For starters, I made sure everything worked.

Think of it like planning a big wedding, only you've got 20,000 guests coming. And another wedding tomorrow and maybe two on Saturday and two more on Sunday.

Sex, drugs, rock 'n roll.

What could go wrong? Uh, let me count the ways.

As general manager of the building, or, in my case, president, I was responsible for over a thousand full- and part-time employees—sometimes seven days a week.

I oversaw these departments:

___

1. **Operations**
   - a. Unions
     - i. Plumbing
     - ii. Carpentry
     - iii. Electrical
     - iv. Ushering
     - v. Painting
     - vi. Staging
     - vii. Sound
     - viii. Lighting
     - ix. Ticketing
     - x. Equipment operators
   - b. Changeover
   - c. Ice management
   - d. Equipment
   - e. Concessions
   - f. Maintenance
   - g. HVAC
   - h. Parking

2. **Finance**
   a. Box Office
   b. Payables
   c. Collectables
   d. Taxes
   e. Payroll
   f. Budgets
   g. Insurance
   h. Event settlements
   i. Banking

3. **Security**
   a. Events
   b. Offices
   c. Dressing rooms
   d. Parking
   e. Talent
   f. Back stage
   g. Doors
   h. Equipment
   i. Box office

4. **Bookings**
   a. Events
   b. Scheduling
   c. Promoters
   d. Hockey
   e. Basketball
   f. Circus
   g. Ice shows
   h. Gymnastics
   i. Tennis
   j. Track
   k. Boxing
   l. Wrestling
   m. Horse shows
   n. Roller derby
   o. Monster trucks

5. **Marketing**
   a. Event advertising
   b. Signage
   c. Public relations
   d. Promotions
   e. Sponsorships
   f. Scoreboard
   g. Suites
   h. Brochures
   i. Printing

Today, there are lots more departments, including:

1. Information technology
2. Social media
3. Human relations
4. Premium seating
5. Analytics
6. Hospitality/guest services
7. External affairs
8. On and on . . .

Back then, excluding team personnel, the Flyers and the 76ers each had those small staffs that I mentioned earlier. Today, the 76ers have some 250 on staff and the hockey team, about as many. Look 'em up on their websites now and they read like telephone books. Remember telephone books?

When you sit in the big office, you pore over every detail before an event, sometimes twice —anticipating the good, the bad and the ugly. You go over everything in your mind, while driving, lying in bed, even on the john. And once again with your staff to be prepared for emergencies, unknowns and some really weird shit that you couldn't imagine, like:

- New drapes in the giant windows catching fire from being bunched too close to high-powered lights.
- Fog obscuring the ice in humid weather.
- The basketball floor being slippery from condensation from ice underneath.
- A sudden roof leak during a downpour.
- Having to cancel an event due to a snowstorm.
- A power failure delaying or prematurely ending an event.
- Hockey glass or a hoops backboard shattering.
- People getting hit with pucks, falling out of the stands, slipping on the steps, fainting, fighting, vomiting, suffering heart and anxiety attacks, overdosing or simply keeling over dead in their seats!

We had a nurse station and an ambulance standing by at most events. At concerts, we also had an M.D. on hand. If someone got bloodied or hurt in a fight or took a tumble, we'd patch them up and have police rush them several blocks away to Saint Agnes Hospital for stitches, X-rays or casts.

Can't tell you how many times I woke up in the middle of the night picturing the huge scoreboard crashing down into the crowd at a concert, or landing on players during a game and closing the building for weeks.

You pretty much know what to expect with hockey and basketball, though we had irate 76ers fans interacting with players and hockey players climbing into the stands to fight abusive guests. If it's college basketball, you've got to handle the kids who had too much beer. If you throw anybody out of any event, make sure you escort them several blocks away, so they don't pick up a rock and break one of the expensive, big plate windows.

If you're doing a giveaway item, make sure you have enough on hand. Once, we ran out of tee shirts before half the fans had entered. Turned out the ushers, security and concession stand workers had grabbed bunches of them before we even opened the doors, nearly creating a riot when the fans streamed in. We fixed that unauthorized practice by giving each event worker one of the items when they showed up for work.

Certain giveaways you do on the way in, like photos or tee shirts. Miniature hockey sticks, souvenir basketballs, soccer balls and pucks you do on the way out, so they don't wind up being thrown on the ice or court if things go south.

What's the makeup of tonight's crowd? Heavy metal head bangers? Goths or meth heads? Hard boxing fans from different Philly neighborhoods? Urban radio station marathon concert devotees?

If it's wrestling, you gotta keep the crazies in the ring and the crazier in the stands. If it's country music or pop and you ask them to move back, they say, "How far?"

I'd try to picture how an entire event would play out from the minute the doors opened to the end of the changeover for the next day. Sometimes, after a late night out, I'd swing by the Spectrum around 1:00 or 2:00 a.m. before heading home. It didn't hurt to have the boss pop in unannounced once in a while.

I'd also have to deal with issues and special requests involving politicians, the media, sponsors, suite owners, season ticket holders, team and building owners and their wives and kids.

One big-name politician had me put his wife in one suite and his girlfriend in another—like across the arena.

I had to make sure the building was booked most every day, so we didn't have too many "dark" nights. Back then, it cost the Spectrum $5,000 a day to operate, so every dark night was a wasted day and five grand down the drain. God knows what it costs the Wells Fargo Center to operate today.

Our head of booking was a sweetheart of a guy, Steve Greenberg, who coordinated all the dates, especially trying to appease the hockey and basketball GMs when it came to not sending them on the road for too many games due to week-long family shows. And not making them play four games in five nights. And not making them play a weekend home matinee after an away game a thousand miles away the night before.

Players don't like being on the road every Christmas or New Year's. Like us, they want to be home with their families, so we'd try not to send them off too often.

The Flyers wanted to play Thursdays and Sundays, with an occasional Saturday or Sunday matinee. The 76ers liked Wednesdays and Fridays with a few Sunday afternoons for national TV. The concert people wanted mostly weekends.

Playoffs were a calendar jigsaw puzzle. We'd lose a bunch of touring concerts in April, May and June, having to block off so many dates for two teams' possible playoff games. The Flyers could miss the playoffs in the final seconds of the final day of the season, as actually once took place, or a dominant 76ers team be eliminated after only two home games, which also happened, or go to the seventh game of the finals, which occasionally happened. It was a total crapshoot.

Booker Greenberg also needed to find or even create new events to fill dates. He'd keep up with other arenas around the world to see what new or unusual events they were presenting.

But thanks to me, we missed something monumentally—globally—big. You can read all about it, and a few other personal bungles, at the end of this book in my Epilogue.

Performing a high-wire act without a net, however, suited my daredevil spirit. I had a blast—but running a beast of an arena could eat you alive!

4

Blood, Sweat & Cheers

Selling Hockey Philly-Style

I walked under the famous arched marquee and into the dank foyer of New York's old Madison Square Garden on 8th Avenue at 49th Street on a crisp Sunday afternoon. It was November 20, 1966, five days short of my 31st birthday—and my present landed in my lap.

"Holy shit," I said, and I whistled, lifting my eyes in awe from the blinding white sheet of ice up to the worn, wooden rafters. It was my first National Hockey League game. The drafty arena, which had opened 41 years earlier and would be torn down in two years for the present building over Penn Station, was aroar with 16,000 hockey nuts in full throat. And this was just the pre-game warm up.

The New York Rangers were about to take on the Montreal Canadiens in what would be a match straight out of hockey heaven. Warming up to the beat of the booming organ were skating gods in swirling symmetry: Jean Beliveau, Henri Richard, Jacques Lemaire, Serge Sevard and Gump Worsley for Montreal, and New York's Rod Gilbert, Jean Ratelle, Phil Goyette and Boom Boom Geffrion. Legendary names, all.

I was but a humble worshiper in a cathedral of hockey.

By the end of the rollicking 20-minute first period, I knew we had a hit on our hands.

"Wait'll Philly sees this," I thought, body and mind buzzed by adrenaline.

The game was a colorful blur of speed and skill as if seen through a kaleidoscope. Hitting and slashing. Bodies, sticks and pucks battering the dasher boards. I stood transfixed. With my face pressed up against the throbbing corner glass, I could literally *feel* this game. Like when you stand on a train platform waiting for the local and the express suddenly thunders by. It was human pinball at warp speed.

With every thump and bump, crash and smash, bodies flying and skates spraying ice, this was a sports mecca gone mad. I knew immediately that Philly fans would go bonkers when they saw it in their shiny new $6-million showplace.

By the end of the second period, I knew exactly how I was going to sell it back home. I scribbled it down in an old, spiraled notebook that I still carried from my days as a reporter:

"A bare-knuckled combination of football and figure skating. Beauty and brutality. Muscle and skill. Flashing blades, iconic uniforms, romantic names. No timeouts. No time to catch your breath. And blood. Lots of blood!"

The constant roar of the frenzied crowd shook the building, deafened the senses and drove the players even harder. Montreal won, 2–1, in a savagely intense contest. With only six teams in the league back then playing one another with frequency, familiarity did indeed breed contempt. I was pumped and exhausted and couldn't wait to rush all this energy and passion 90 miles down the turnpike. If I, "Mr. Cool," was hooked, the fans would be too.

I saw several other NHL games before the Flyers would play their first regular season game ever, almost a year later—a 5–1 opening day loss in Oakland against the California Seals on October 11, 1967. A personal thrill was having dinner before that game at the Oakland Alameda County Arena with Ed Snider and Seals' minority owner Charles Schulz, of *Peanuts* fame.

But months earlier, in the huge, jammed Chicago Stadium, I watched the Blackhawks physically punish the Detroit Red Wings. At the fabled old Montreal Forum, *Les Habs* shut out the despised Toronto Maple Leafs in a bloody brawl of a contest with nationalistic survival seemingly at stake. After a trip to a Boston Bruins game at the decrepit old Boston Garden, I had now seen the six teams that had comprised the NHL since 1942.

Six new teams, including Philly's, would be added in the first-ever expansion of the NHL, the others being St. Louis, Oakland, Minnesota, Pittsburgh and Los Angeles. Vancouver was shut out and a bitterly disappointed Baltimore group was designated the first alternate.

What we had here were helmetless warriors, hair flying behind them, possessed goalies without face masks, stitched-up skaters with mocking smiles and nasty attitudes pounding one another. Bloodletting was a badge of honor.

I knew this game would sell to both Philly's blue-collar crowd *and* the Broad Street CEOs. But what about women? Would they go for it?

I took note of the crowd's makeup at the NHL arenas and realized the game held more than a subtle fascination for women. More than one quarter of the attendance was female. This inspired the thought that if I could sell the game to the ladies, not only would their men be allowed to come to the building more often, but the ladies would attend as well. Hockey sells. Sex sells. Tickets sell.

At one of these early games I whipped out my trusty notebook again, and sketched a theme that eventually led to a series of intriguing newspaper ads that I ran in what then was called the "Women's Section" of area newspapers:

**There are deep psychological reasons
why so many women love hockey.**

Find out for yourself!

FLYERS VS. PITTSBURGH

7:05 pm Thursday, October 12, 1967
The Spectrum HO 5 4500

Seeing women viscerally react to the spectacle of a fist fight on ice and to the bedlam of a hard-earned goal made me think they might subconsciously feel these bladed gladiators were fighting over them. And the victor, some women may fantasize, won them. Men have been fighting over women since before fire was invented. In the animal world it's called the mating ritual.

Hey, I was hired to sell a sport in a town that thought icing was something butter-scotched atop a TastyKake Krimpet®.

There's an arousal power in violence—and people are drawn to it. The game, I reasoned, was a fascinating sexual being of its own. Here were tough men, muscular and menacing, chasing an elusive quarry of a three-inch, vulcanized rubber puck across a 17,000-square-foot frozen sheet, banging away at the enemy's harried goalie, who was desperately defending the honor of his net.

Bang! Thrust! Slam! Pound! They buzzed the goalie, persisting with sticks, elbows and knees in an onslaught so unrelenting that it had you standing, jumping and screaming until hoarse—begging for the ultimate release.

Finally ... Achingly ... Oh, my God ... Thankfully . . . S-C-O-R-E!

The puck penetrates the mouth of the goal, the vanquished goalie sprawls exhausted, the building explodes. Players hug. Strangers embrace. Lights flash. Hats fly. Confetti. Sirens. Stands tremble. Pandemonium. A fucking tsunami of ecstasy. The climax of a lifetime. Sweet Jesus!

Rapture for the home heroes. Despair for the evil invaders.

Settling back in our seats, spent and panting, you could almost feel the mob enjoying a post-climactic cigarette.

"Women are gonna love it," I reflected. "And a lot of guys are gonna get lucky."

5

A Dozen Jock Straps

76ers Show Some Balls

The turkey was picked clean and the annual pumpkin pie from Horn & Hardarts' was history. It was Thanksgiving, 1948. My thirteenth birthday.

I gave my mom, dad and sister quick kisses, grabbed my weathered leather jacket—a Gimbels basement special with the fake shearling collar—and headed out the door. Taking two trolley cars at night from our candy store at 30th Street and Girard Avenue to the old Arena at 46th & Market was no big deal for a kid back then.

The Philly Warriors were playing the Washington Capitols—yes, spelled with an "o"—and I couldn't wait to see my heroes: Joe Fulks, George Senesky, Howie Dallmar, Ed Sadowski and Angelo Musi. That they lost, 81–73, didn't matter. It was the early days of pro basketball, and I was in love with my Philly team. Jumpin' Joe Fulks, a lanky Kentucky boy, was pioneering something called a jump shot. The silky Senesky was an All American at St. Joe's, and Musi was a skinny 5'9" guard out of Temple. Eddie "The Mogul" Gottlieb, another Philly guy, was GM and coach.

"Gotty" eventually purchased the team from owner Pete Tyrell, and we had some pretty good years with legends Guy Rodgers from Temple by way of Northeast High School and Overbrook's Wilt Chamberlain, before Gottlieb ripped my heart out in 1962 by selling the franchise to West Coast investors who planted it in San Francisco. Yeah, that's your Golden State Warriors today, fans!

We even celebrated two Warriors' championships: In 1947 in the Basketball Association of America, a year before the National

33

Basketball Association was formed, and the NBA crown in 1956. Wilt scored those legendary 100 points against the New York Knicks in March 1962, in a Warriors "home" game at Hershey, PA, with the great playmaker Rodgers piling up 20 assists.

That was the team's final year here, as we were stunned a few months after the season by its sale. Gottlieb pocketed $850,000, a handsome sum for an NBA franchise at the time.

So Philadelphia was without an NBA team for a year until Ike Richman, a prominent Philly lawyer, and investor Irv Kosloff, a paper manufacturer, bought the NBA's Syracuse Nationals for about $500,000 and moved the team to Philadelphia. Richman and Kosloff had been classmates at South Philadelphia High School and Richman was Wilt's attorney. The owners held a contest to rename the team "the 76ers," who played at the old Arena and Convention Hall with an occasional game at Penn's historic Palestra.

Richman died suddenly of a heart attack in 1965 at age 52 while sitting behind the 76ers' bench at a Celtics playoff game at old Boston Garden. Shockingly, some members of Ike's family watching back home witnessed it on television.

Kosloff, the reserved, silent partner, reluctantly took charge.

In April 1967, five months before the Spectrum was to open, the 76ers won the NBA championship defeating—you guessed it—those San Francisco Warriors. That 76ers team is considered one of the greatest NBA teams ever, with a gaudy 68–13 record led by coach Alex Hannum and stars Chamberlain, Hal Greer and Billy Cunningham.

The following year, with the Spectrum fully under construction, Ed Snider and I began negotiating with Kosloff and his lawyer, Nate Budin, to have his team join the Flyers as a co-tenant at the Spectrum. Irv politely explained he was a conservative guy who liked things simple. "I don't need higher rent in a flashy new building," he said. But after a few weeks of sometimes tense talks, Irv was ready to "talk gesheft," the Yiddish term for business.

Irv and I had a great rapport right off the bat, while Ed Snider was all business. Good cop, bad cop stuff.

"What do you really think?" Irv leaned over and asked me when Ed headed to the restroom. Ed was frustrated by the drawn-out negotiations and said earlier that as far as he was concerned, this was going to be a take-it-or-leave-it session.

"Irv," I said, "you can't afford not to be a part of this new building. You've got to show basketball fans, the press and the city that the 76ers are first class."

As Ed returned, I shot him a look that said things were looking good.

"I'll make sure you get the same terms as the Flyers," I said.

Budin said they'd want a copy of the hockey team's lease.

"Of course," I said, as Ed rolled his eyes.

Irv looked at his lawyer and nodded.

"Okay," Irv said, adding, "Just a small office and a room big enough to hold a dozen jock straps."

Relieved, to finally get his signature on the lease, I carved out space below the stands for a handful of offices next to the Flyers' larger HQ and dedicated one of the larger locker rooms nearby for a few more "jock straps" than he requested. I kind of knew they'd grow into it.

Kosloff was a successful businessman and turned out to be an astute team owner, allowing canny general manager Pat Williams to wheel and deal in the player market and lure crowds with zany promotions and elaborate half-time shows. Pat was a ringmaster of promotions and he loved the Spectrum's acoustics. "It was ear-shattering," he said. The sound in the Spectrum was great, but when we added the third deck under the roof in 1972, the sound totally blasted off it.

■ ■ ■

Legendary Dave Zinkoff was the team's long-time, theatrical public address announcer whose shticks included giving away lucky number program prizes of Hebrew National Salamis and teasing the crowd with amusing announcements of cars in the parking lot "with headlights beaming, engine on and windshield wipers running." He'd give out a questionable license plate number and finish with a crowd-groaning, "...and the *dooorrs* are locked!"

He called Wilt's hellacious throwdowns "Dippperrrr Dunks!" and introduced Dr. J. as "Julius Errrrrrrving!" When the 76ers' Gene Shue would go to the foul line in the early '70s, before becoming a coach, the "Zink" would chirp, "Shue [pause] for two!" When LaSalle and Warriors' NBA hall of famer Tom Gola hit a basket, Dave would yell "Gola Goal!!"

The Zink was a riot. Short in stature, he loved to squire taller show-girl types around town, perhaps as beards. He and Eddie Gottlieb, both bachelors, went to their graves as close friends—perhaps more, as their contemporary, Harvey "Super Stat" Pollack, surprisingly remarked at the dedication of a Pennsylvania Historical Marker honoring "Gotty" outside South Philadelphia High School at Broad and Snyder.

The Zink was a nice Jewish boy whose parents wanted him to be a lawyer, a doctor or a CPA, but he turned out to be one of the most famous voices in the history of professional basketball.

Before he was the voice of the 76ers, he announced Philadelphia Warriors games, traveled internationally with the Harlem Globetrotters and (prior to that) worked with Gottlieb as an announcer for the Philadelphia Sphas. At Temple, he announced at boxing matches and the Owls basketball games. He announced the first Sugar Bowl game in New Orleans in 1935, where coach Pop Warner's Temple team lost a close one to Tulane. He also did Phillies games at Connie Mack Stadium, becoming one of the most recognizable voices in sports. Dave rejected overtures from other cities, vowing to never leave his beloved Philadelphia. He continued behind the microphone as public address announcer for the 76ers until passing away in 1985.

GM Williams once brought in Victor the Wrestling Bear for a half-time show and convinced Vince Papale, the Eagles' walk-on hero and later inspiration for Disney's *Invincible* movie, to get in a ring with the animal. Papale rushed him, and the bear walloped him across the face. There was a lot of blood. "My tooth came up through my lip," said Vince, "and I ended up getting five stitches in the Sixers' locker room. But I felt so cool. I felt like a hockey player."

Philly sports talk guy Howard Eskin likes to tell people about the time Pat Williams asked him what he could do to get him to mud-wrestle after a game. "There were a lot of beautiful cheerleaders, and I said, 'If I can wrestle this one, I'd be happy to do it.'" Eskin promoted the mud thing during the game and got the fans going. "I'm pumping up the crowd, and the cheerleader's out there. Now it's after the game, and all of a sudden, no cheerleader—just two professional mud-wrestlers. I mean, these women had to be 300 pounds apiece. Gigantic. I had to go through with it."

"One of the finest moments in sports history," Williams says with a straight face. "Howard would tell you that he dominated, but I think the two women ganged up on him." "I pinned both of them," quoth the man known and revered as "Humble Howard."

Eskin also was the Spectrum ring announcer for a World Wrestling Federation event with Hulk Hogan and the Million Dollar Man. The match was over, or at least Eskin thought so, and he jumped into the ring to announce the winner. Hulk told him, "Brother, you better get the fuck out of here!" The match was over, but it wasn't over. Eskin jumped back out of the ring, and they went at it again.

"I've spent some serious time [there], brother," Hogan recalled in a *Philadelphia Magazine* piece about the Spectrum. "There's folding metal chairs in all these buildings that we used to swing and hit each other with. At the Spectrum, the chairs have padding, and it makes them probably 20 pounds heavier. Mr. Wonderful, Paul Orndorff, once hit me with a chair and just knocked me cold.

"I came to in the middle of the ring, and I asked the referee, 'Where am I?' And he said, 'You're in the Spectrum.' I got through the match, went back to the dressing room, and was so dazed and confused that I didn't even get a shower. I don't remember walking to my car. I always used to stop at this Burger King a few blocks away. I found myself in the parking lot, sitting with my wrestling boots and my tights on, and I couldn't think of how I got there."

Sorry to digress, but thought you'd like to hear these Spectrum nuggets.

■ ■ ■

In 1976, Irv Kosloff sold the 76ers to socialite F. Eugene Dixon, Jr. for $8 million. "Fitz" Dixon, an inheritor of the local blue-blood Widener and Elkins family fortunes, had owned pieces of Philly teams but yearned for his own team.

"It was an itch I wanted to scratch for years," he said.

In two years, under Fitz and with coach Billy Cunningham, the 76ers were a championship-caliber team featuring Julius Erving, Mo Cheeks, Doug Collins, Bobby Jones and Darryl Dawkins. At Pat Williams' urging, Fitz acquired Doctor J after Pat patiently explained who Erving was and what he'd mean to the team.

Fitz bought Erving's contract for $3 million in 1976 from the struggling New York Nets of the rival American Basketball Association, which eventually merged with the NBA. Erving would go on to lead the 76ers to four NBA finals and a championship in 1983, their last championship.

But in 1980 they weren't drawing well, averaging fewer than 11,000 fans per game in the 18,000-seat Spectrum, pathetic for a pedigreed team that won 59 games and lost only 23. There was a serious disconnect with the fans. The team was bleeding money and Dixon decided the club needed someone to spark fan support. My days as Ed Snider's lieutenant were waning at this point, and when Snider heard about the opening, he eagerly suggested me as a candidate.

First, I met with Dixon's lawyer, Peter Matoon, who, after a vetting process, recommended me to Fitz as someone with the credentials and experience to change the 76ers dynamic.

I flew to the Dixon winter estate in Florida, situated on a private island off old-money Palm Beach. At dinner at his private club,

Matoon, Fitz and his wife, Edith, peppered me with questions. I told them I would come on board only if I had full authority to run things and that Fitz had to take my advice——whether he agreed with it or not.

"Otherwise," I said, "We'll both be wasting our time."

The team was elite, but Dixon was not popular, sitting courtside under the east basket with guards blocking fans from walking past in front. I was told he even kicked one fan in the ass who eluded a guard.

I said he needed to stop playing Nero and relocate his entourage to a box off the floor. The press and most fans, especially the Blacks, who stayed away in droves, saw him as pushy, petulant and privileged. This has to change, I told Fitz. "It starts at the top." As Ed Snider liked to say, "Fish stink from the head."

At breakfast the next morning on his lush, tropical patio facing the Atlantic Ocean, Dixon told me the position of team president was mine—with full control.

"The world's your oyster, kid," he said. "Don't fuck it up."

Edith added a warning: "He'll fire you a few times—but hire you right back." That actually came true one time, which I'll get to in a bit.

Fitz said the team was losing about $4 million a year and hoped I could fix it so that he "didn't have to dip into my principal." Coming from the fiscally austere Snider organization, I assured Fitz that losing money was not in my DNA.

I have to credit Ed Snider for helping me land this job. He deftly eased me out—and into a great spot.

"I don't want to hurt your feelings," Ed's first wife, Myrna, confided at dinner one night. "But he 'sold you' like others he didn't think he needed anymore."

I loved Myrna like a sister, maybe more, and appreciated her sharing this, but I wasn't insulted in the least—nor surprised. I knew Ed's *modus operandi* six ways from Sunday.

"We both got what we wanted," I said.

Myrna was a dear friend with whom I remained close until she passed on May 22, 2014 at age 78. Lung cancer caught up with her after years of smoking and sailing under the sun. Everyone loved Myrna. She was beautiful, sweet, warm and fun. Plus, she could throw a football twenty yards—in a tight spiral. Her identical twin sister, Dobbie (who passed away at age 84, in December 2020, due to complications of leukemia), was quieter and more demure than the free-spirited, heart-of-a-gypsy Myrna. Dobbie was just as sweet and beautiful. Together, they were a dynamo.

They did everything from making the players' families welcome to helping design staff uniforms to decorating the team and arena facilities. Myrna was a genuine and welcome figure in the Spectrum, greeting secretaries, ushers, players and execs, brightening up our lives on almost a daily basis. She was the glue who made everyone feel like family.

Ed died two years after Myrna on April 11, 2016, battling every step of the way as bladder cancer ravaged his system. Ed and the twins are buried a few hundred yards apart in West Laurel Hill Cemetery in Lower Merion. Ed's grave sports a Flyers logo, his true love, and Myrna's, a figure of a sailboat. She loved life on the sea—as well as the boat's captain, Martin Thomas—a modest, soft-spoken Brit—whom she went on to marry.

Taking over as president of the 76ers, I genuinely liked Fitz Dixon. He could be petty and tart-tongued, but he treated me well and heeded my advice. We got along fine, even the time he fired me—and, as Edith predicted, rehired me.

Before we get to that, I have to relate an incident where Fitz put me on the spot in front of his friends, and I had to put him in his place. I had been checking out the building as per usual before the doors opened for a 76ers game, and so I walked into the Owner's Lounge later than usual. With a drink swishing in his hand, Fitz greeted me rudely and loudly.

"Where you been, you little prick?" he cracked for everyone to hear.

The room hushed.

He stood there cockily, with a hand on a hip and a smirk on his face. His Episcopal Academy prep tie was tucked into his pants with a leather belt cinched high above his waist. It may have been fun to him to talk to the help like that, but I wasn't about to take it.

"Fitz," I shot back, jabbing a finger toward his chest, "I told you before, don't *ever* . . . call me *little!*"

"Touché," Fitz responded, nearly doubling over in laughter.

His guests roared. Message delivered.

Months before, when I first moved into the 76ers' handsome new offices on the ground level of Veterans Stadium, where they had relocated from their sparse Spectrum quarters across Pattison Avenue, first thing Fitz did was install a red telephone in my office. Yes, a red phone!

"This is *my* phone," he said in clipped tones. "It is for *me* to call *you*. If anyone else ever answers, they are fired. If I call and there's a busy signal, you're fired."

I would see Fitz often, at every home game, on some road trips, at team social events and when he visited the offices every couple of weeks, so there was no acute need for the "Bat Phone."

Until one day . . .

It was a hectic afternoon, a few hours before a critical home play-off game against the Boston Celtics. I needed to make an urgent call and all the office lines were tied up. I looked at the red phone, said "fuck it!" and dialed David Stern, then NBA vice president, at league headquarters in New York. I was on the NBA negotiating committee for league radio and TV rights and we were in final talks for a major new contract. David and I had become close, and we were pushing for a league payday in the emerging world of cable TV.

Sure enough, the one stinkin' time I'm on that phone is the one stinkin' time Fitz calls. What are the odds? I was on it for maybe five minutes. Soon as I hang up, it rings. It's Fitz and he's furious, demanding to know why *his* phone is being used. Before I could reply, he shouts, "You're fired!" I hang up, steam for a minute—and go back to work.

About an hour later, it rings again.

"You still there?" he asks.

"I am."

"Fine."

Guess I just got rehired.

Later at the game, he doesn't mention it and neither do I. All in a day's work.

Fitz did a lot of great things for Philadelphia. One of the most meaningful was his anonymous purchase of the popular *Love* sculpture that Robert Indiana had loaned to the city for the 1976 Bicentennial celebration. The Rizzo regime, no appreciators of art, made such a last-minute, lowball offer to purchase it that Indiana, who felt it belonged in the City of Brotherly Love, reluctantly sent a truck and hauled it back to New York. The Indiana family gallery said the token offer, less than what it cost to make it, was insulting.

Fitz, who also was chairman of the Philadelphia Art Commission, was furious when he found out—as were thousands of residents and visitors who showed up for wedding and proposal photo-ops and found the statue gone. Dixon immediately called City Hall.

"Buy *Love!*" he directed one of Rizzo's commissioners. "Get it back here where it belongs. Whatever it costs, I'll pay for it."

Fitz shelled out $35,000 and donated it to the city. "I don't want any publicity on this," he told me. Eventually, word of his grand gesture surfaced, and he was persuaded to take part in a ceremony with

Rizzo at 15th Street and JFK Boulevard, where it famously resides today in what is known as "Love Park."

Running the 76ers organization and trying to promote bigger crowds was a tough job. Long hours, seven days a week and a lot of travel—to away games; league meetings in New York, LA and Florida; business trips to Chicago, Houston and Atlanta to woo or placate sponsors.

The fans mostly were unmoved, the hold-over office staff members were skeptical of my style and the basketball press privately slammed me as "a hockey guy."

I got ripped the first night on the job by the *Daily News'* veteran basketball writer Jack Kiser. We'd just beaten, I think, the Detroit Pistons in a sloppy game, and on my way out of the Spectrum, Ed, the long-time security guard, congratulated me on the win.

"Yeah," I threw out, "Great win. Thanks."

Kiser, within earshot, later told his newspaper colleagues that I was praising a lousy win as a great win and rode me and my efforts hard after that. As far as I'm concerned, any fucking win is a great fucking win!

Aggressive marketing, reaching out to the Black community and improving the game-day experience for the fans made only slight gains during my two seasons on the job.

The first season, 1979–80, we went to the finals but lost four games to two to the Los Angeles Lakers. The sixth game of that series was at the Spectrum and we needed to win, tie the series at three apiece and go back to L.A. for game seven. When word came that Lakers' star center Kareem Abdul Jabbar was not making the trip due to an injury or migraines, we were stoked. But a rookie forward by the name of Ervin Johnson moved to center, magically played all five positions, racked up 42 points and 15 rebounds and we were eliminated. Not sure what became of Ervin after that.

Fitz was not a happy camper.

The following year, we went a sparkling 62–20, but were embarrassed in the conference finals by the hated Boston Celtics, ignominiously blowing a three-games-to-one series lead. Worse, Boston went on to win the NBA championship and Fitz decided he'd had enough. His lawyer, Matoon, told me they'd decided to sell the team and were declining to renew my contract for another 18 months "to allow a new owner to pick his own guy."

The new owner turned out to be Harold Katz, a native of South Philadelphia and founder of Nutri-Systems, who purchased the franchise for "a shade over $12 million."

Fifteen years later, in 1996, hyper-energetic Novacare founder Pat Croce maneuvered a deal to have Comcast buy the 76ers from Katz plus purchase two-thirds of Ed Snider's Spectacor company. Croce reportedly anted up about $5 million to own about 2.5 percent of the pie and got to run the 76ers as president.

Katz loved owning the 76ers and really didn't want to sell, but Croce—and a cool $125 million from Comcast—wore him down.

The 76ers were pretty bad at the time following disastrous drafts, trades and PR gaffes, and Katz was feeling the heat of the fans and media.

"It's a sad day for me," he said at the press conference, adding that Croce drove him nuts, "Calling me to ask, 'Are you ready? Are you ready? Are you ready?'"

"I'm not even ready today," said a clearly pained Katz.

The blockbuster deal was a mega payoff for Snider, as Comcast reportedly paid $250 million in cash and stock to get two-thirds of Snider's Spectacor and assumed two-thirds of the renamed Comcast Spectacor's $180 million overall debt.

Snider retained one-third of everything, including that of the acquired 76ers, with authority to run the whole shebang. Some say his annual compensation was as much as $25 million. He had taken on considerable debt in the $210 million construction of his new arena, then called Corestates Center, and confided to friends he was concerned about the risk. This bailed him out, and then some! It was like a guy in a leaking rowboat being thrown a yacht.

In effect, he cashed out—but stayed in.

The pile of dough, the annual take and the relief of debt was great, but the Comcast stock was a godsend. Appreciation and splits over the next 20 years resulted in staggering numbers.

While Croce had done the leg work, the maven credited with making it happen was center city real estate baron Ron Rubin, a close friend of Snider's and owner of the Bellevue Hotel, the former Gallery on Market Street, and lots more. Snider had told Rubin he was worried. Ron, aiming to make a marriage, pitched the idea to his friend Ralph Roberts, then head of Comcast. Ralph and son Brian immediately saw the wonders of sports programming and co-promotions with the entertainment center. Rubin, a quiet, respected figure in Philadelphia power circles for decades, then introduced Croce to Ralph Roberts. Rubin passed away in April 2021 at age 89. I was lucky to have lunch with him at the Palm Restaurant in the Bellevue shortly before it closed in 2020, during which he filled me in.

Much of the attraction to Comcast was that Snider would stay in control. Comcast wanted nothing to do with the day-to-day operations. This was a smart investment by the Robertses in their hometown, but small potatoes on Comcast's mammoth balance sheet.

And it catapulted Snider into the realm of the super wealthy. Free of financial concern and more than set for life, he took on his new role in running Comcast Spectacor, his sparkling new arena and the basketball franchise, lighter of step and with renewed vigor and enthusiasm.

Croce ran the 76ers with his hair on fire for five years, but wanted bigger fish to fry. He told Snider what he really wanted was Ed's job. But Ed liked things just the way they were and told Pat to chill, which is like telling a runaway forest fire nearing Ed's California mansion to simmer down. Croce unwisely went public with his desires, indicating Snider was stepping down, and an irate Snider just as publicly slapped him down. After that, Ed gave Croce the cold treatment and Pat eventually resigned.

Snider handled stewardship of the basketball club for the next 15 years, juggling time and energy between the teams. By 2011, with the struggling 76ers needing a complete dismantling and the rest of his empire demanding full attention, he decided to jettison the franchise. "I don't have the stomach to tear the team down and go through a rebuilding process," he told me.

The team was sold for a bargain price of $287 million to a group headed by billionaire Josh Harris of New York, a savvy Wharton grad who co-founded Apollo Global Management, which buys distressed properties and turns them around. And boy, did he and his partner, David Blitzer, another Wharton boychik, turn this one around!

The basketball franchise, as a tenant with a stiff lease at the Wells Fargo Center and little to no revenue from in-house advertising, parking or concessions, was valued by Forbes in February 2021 at more than $2.1 billion, seven and one-half times the sale price.

Harris and Blitzer want their own arena when the current lease expires in 2031, maybe sooner. Their company, Harris Blitzer Sports and Entertainment, already owns the NHL New Jersey Devils and soccer teams in Europe and controls the Prudential Center in Newark. HBSE has looked into buying an NFL franchise and took a run at purchasing the New York Mets.

A proposal by Harris and Blitzer to build an arena on the Philly waterfront at Penn's Landing quickly was shot down by the Delaware River Waterfront Corporation in favor of a sweeping, family-and pedestrian-friendly renewal plan submitted by the Durst Organization, a large New York real estate developer. The 76ers say they want to stay in Philly, but own acres of land next to their complex of offices and practice facilities in Camden, which makes for intriguing possibilities even though Trenton isn't giving away land and tax credits like Daddy Warbucks anymore.

Comcast Spectacor just poured $300 million into heavy upgrades at the Wells Fargo Center to stay abreast of the hospitality curve, and another $11 million for COVID-19 protection. The return on that 2011 sale of the 76ers, in retrospect, doesn't sit well at the bodacious Comcast towers in center city. Nor did the unanticipated losses due to the extended pandemic shutdown of the big arena.

The cable giant is used to making tough, elbow-sharp deals on an international basis—and it's no secret it would love to have a mulligan on that 76ers sale. If Brian Roberts decides to unload the whole shootin' match, a possibility that's more than a whisper, you can be sure he'll fight tooth and nail to make up for undervaluing the franchise.

And how sweet would it be if the buyers sitting across the negotiation table just happen to be the aforementioned Wharton Wunderkinds?

6

Wolman vs. Snider

Damon Battles Pythias

It's said there are three sides to every story. This one has a fourth . . . mine. I came to, sore and groggy, in a room at Philly's Einstein Hospital near Broad Street and Olney Avenue following surgery in December 1963 for a meniscus I ripped playing Sunday-morning sandlot football.

First thing I focus on is a grainy, black-and-white TV suspended from the ceiling. Channel 6 anchor Gunnar Back, I think, was introducing film of two guys I had never heard of who had just bought the Philadelphia Eagles.

It was ten days after JFK was shot, and the first time I laid eyes on Ed Snider and Jerry Wolman, sharp young Washington, DC guys who shocked local Philly *machers* by snatching the team put up for sale by a Philly group known as "the Hundred Brothers."

This investor group, which owned the team from 1949 to 1963, was headed by local trucking magnate James P. Clark and the politically connected Philly Fire Chief Frank McNamee, who also was the team president. They had rounded up 100 Philadelphia backers who forked over $3000 each to buy the team from cash-strapped owner Alexis 'Lex' Thompson for $250,000 plus operating cash to make sure it remained in the city.

Out of the hospital and back on the beat covering City Hall for the *Philadelphia Daily News*, I soon meet Jerry Wolman at a 1964 press conference in the Eagles' swank offices on the ground floor of the *Evening Bulletin* Building at 30th and Market Streets.

Wolman was involved in a nasty dispute with Mayor James H. J. Tate over a signed agreement granting the Eagles "exclusive professional football rights" to play in Veterans Stadium, planned for the Eagles and Phillies in South Philadelphia, which was to open in 1971.

Wolman wrote in his 2010 book, *Jerry Wolman: The World's Richest Man*, that he was summoned to Tate's City Hall office and blindsided with a concocted lease that not only jacked up the rent but disaffirmed the "exclusive" pro football clause. What's more, it directed that the Eagles would play in a stadium to be built on stilts over Pennsylvania Railroad tracks at 30th Street Station, not the South Philly site at Broad Street and Pattison Avenue.

Wolman said he was told by Tate and his gang that he had no choice but to sign on the spot because that's the way it worked in Philly—and he'd better get used to it. They warned him that if he didn't go along, the city could pressure the University of Pennsylvania to kick the Eagles out of their current home at Franklin Field on Penn's campus.

Now, Wolman may have come from poor folks who owned a grocery store in down-and-out Shenandoah, PA, but he didn't exactly just fall off the back of a turnip truck. He was a savvy, successful developer who, at age 36, was said to be worth $36 million the day he bought the Eagles.

Digging into the story, I learned Tate was courting a rival franchise from the budding American Football League to share the new stadium with the Eagles and Phillies. I also heard rumors that Tate might personally benefit if the AFL franchise wound up playing in the new stadium.

Tate and his cohorts thought they had the young owner trapped, but Wolman pulled an end run. He went out and bought Connie Mack Stadium, née Shibe Park, where the Eagles had played before moving to Franklin Field. Connie Mack Stadium was the long-time home of the Phillies. Team owner Robert R. M. Carpenter, an heir to the DuPont family, had unloaded the old ballpark about a year earlier to New York real estate investors.

Wolman said he walked out of Tate's office seething, placed a call to New York and "in a ten-minute conversation," bought the stadium for $575,000. Moving quickly, Wolman rounded up Carpenter and said the Phillies could play there so long as they wanted, along with the Eagles. Then, he and Carpenter would build their own stadium somewhere. Wolman called a press conference and went public with Tate's strong-arm tactics.

Outfoxed by Wolman and dogged by my news articles, Tate caved and dropped talk of an AFL franchise—as well as the ill-advised 30th Street Station site.

Wolman had won the Eagles with an offer of $5,505,000, easily outbidding other suitors, which netted the "brothers'" more than $50,000 each for their $3,000 investments. The minimum bid had been set by the owners at $4.5 million, and the few other applicants reportedly came in not much higher. Asked why he bid so high, Wolman said simply, "Because I fucking wanted to win!"

Wolman, boyish and charismatic, soon introduced me to Ed Snider, 31, an astute, no-nonsense businessman and CPA who had moved from Washington with his family as the Eagles' executive vice president and treasurer, motivated by a 15-year contract, 7 percent ownership of the team and *carte blanche* to run it. As time passed, he and Wolman offered me executive positions in their budding empire.

In short order, Wolman, a developer of major projects in and around the nation's capital, announced a $100-million "City Within a City" development of homes, offices, hospitality and parks on Camden's north shore (which never got off the drawing boards due to funding), purchased Philly's Yellow Cab Co., opened restaurants and clubs in town, helped launch NFL Films and began construction on the John Hancock skyscraper in Chicago.

But I loved the rush of chasing a good story. Being a reporter was my life's dream. Where else could I make a good guy or break a bad one—and read all about it in the morning?

I got into the newspaper business in 1957, dropping out of Temple University's School of Journalism in my senior year to support my wife and daughter, and landed a job writing obituaries at the *Trentonian* (in Trenton). I was in heaven, earning $75 a week and loving every minute. After a few months, they promoted me to general assignment, then City Hall reporter and onto the city desk.

Over the next seven years, I worked at the *Doylestown Intelligencer* in the seat of Bucks County, PA, and at the *Courier Post* in Cherry Hill, NJ. The work was exciting and fulfilling and it came easily to me. In Doylestown, I had the honor of sitting at a desk next to famed author James Michener, a newspaperman at heart, who lived nearby and came in regularly to bang out his new book, *Hawaii*.

At each paper I advanced quickly but was eager to move on to the Big Time. I constantly pestered the *Philly Inquirer, Evening Bulletin* and *Daily News* for a job, but got nowhere.

Then, I got an idea.

The *Bulletin*, which moved to 30th Street from across from City Hall in 1954, was giving tours of its new building. I showed up for one, and when we passed the editorial department, ducked into a men's room, waited a few minutes, navigated a sea of staff desks and found the office of city editor Early Selby.

His door was open, and I could hear the rat-a-tat of a newsman's typewriter.

I poked my head in.

"Mr. Selby?"

He looked up.

"Who are you?"

"Uh, my name's Scheinfeld, and I would love to work for you."

"How'd you get in here?"

I told him; he laughed and invited me in.

He asked about my experience, but said, "We don't have any openings right now, but if we did, I'd hire you, just for figuring out how to get in here. That's the mark of a good newsman."

I could never get past the guard in the tiny lobby of the *Inquirer* on Broad Street but made so many trips to the *Daily News* offices in an old warehouse at 22nd and Arch Streets that city editor Bill Blitman knew me well.

"Kid," he swore each time I showed up, "next opening, you're in!"

True to his word, Bill called me one day and said to give notice at the *Courier Post*. I started at the *Daily News* in September 1963, on the 11p.m.–7a.m. "Lobster Shift" on rewrite, meaning I took raw info over the phone from our night beat reporters at police and fire departments or out covering general news and wrote their stories. Within six months I was assigned to the coveted daytime City Hall beat after a colleague left, and I thrived. I loved this job and couldn't get enough. Breaking one big story after another, my peers dubbed me "Front Page Lou."

But two years into the City Hall beat, I was ordered by crusty old managing editor J. Ray Hunt to move inside as night city editor. It meant going back on the late shift with no pay increase and giving up all the key contacts I had cultivated around town.

I balked. Hunt said either take it or leave! So I made him an offer. I'd take the inside night job *and* work the day shift at City Hall.

I was floored when Hunt said okay.

Even more surprisingly, I not only got paid for covering City Hall — but time-and-a-half overtime for working the 7:00 p.m.–3:00 a.m. night shift. My pay ballooned from $14,000 ($111,000 in today's money) to $22,000 ($176,000 today).

One day, after doing the double shift for almost a year, my phone rang in the City Hall Administration Reporters Room 212. It was Wolman. He said they were working on a big deal and would I have lunch with Snider about something "that's going to knock your socks off."

I met Ed a few days later at Lou Mayo's intimate Bellevue Court lounge behind the Bellevue-Stratford Hotel where, over Bloody Marys and shrimp cocktails, he told me they were applying for a franchise in the National Hockey League and would need to build and operate a new arena if they got it. I thought he was giving me a scoop, but soon realized it was bigger than that.

"How'd you like to help run that?" he asked. Whoa! How do you turn this down?

"If you get the franchise," I said, "I'm on board."

Sure enough, a few weeks later I got the call. "We got it," said Ed. "You in?"

"I'm in," I said without hesitation.

How could you not be impressed with these quicksilver guys? They blew into town like Dodge City gunslingers and dusted off the movers and shakers with style and class. They had damn-the-torpedoes spirit and a seemingly indestructible friendship. Damon and Pythias, I had called them in print. "Wolman sparkled like a chromed guitar in a window of nineteenth-century violins," said one Philly writer.

Much as I loved newspapers, this was a lifetime opportunity—to create a hockey team and build and run an arena. Figuring how to make all of it work in a non-hockey city was a challenge I just had to take on.

In April 1966, I became vice president of the yet unnamed "Hockey Team" and of "The New Sports Arena." In a short matter of time, this kid from a little candy store in Brewerytown would be sitting in a fancy office helping run a big-time hockey team and a big-city arena.

It was heady and exciting, but things spun downhill fast! I watched from an uncomfortable front-row seat as the Wolman–Snider friendship deteriorated into all-out war.

Snider was running the Eagles, honchoing the birth of the hockey team and getting the arena up and running.

Wolman was practically living on commercial jets to and from Chicago, where construction of his $100-million John Hancock Building was going badly, due to a faulty foundation. John Hancock, a conservative Boston company, wanted no part of the political mess roiling in Chicago and pulled its financing.

Jerry poured more than $20 million of his own cash into ripping down several stories of steel superstructure and redoing the concrete underpinning. Turned out that the concrete wasn't given enough time to cure before steel beams were laid on it. When he ran out of dough, Wolman began looking for funding here, there, and everywhere, reportedly eyeing Eagles revenues. Word spread fast. Alarmed creditors soon were howling at the door.

Meanwhile, Snider was running the Eagles by day and working with our staff on the hockey and arena projects at night. Weekdays, he'd arrive at our 15th Street offices around 6:00 p.m. to discuss and strategize the status of things for four or five hours. I called it "Countdown to Opening" and created special memo paper and posters. We'd have long meetings and conference calls on weekends.

By now, Wolman knew he had to dump everything else he owned to try to save his beloved Eagles, and frantically rainbowed from Vegas to Paris to Switzerland, seeking that pot of gold to save his empire.

It looked to us that Wolman, admittedly exhausted and stressed, was unraveling in a last-ditch effort to find money, reportedly dealing with shadowy characters in Vegas, "African princes" and finally an Arab sheik purportedly dangling a $43-million package for his assets, including the Spectrum and the Flyers. Wolman asked Snider and others to give back his gifts of equity in the team and arena so he could package it all in the alleged Arab deal.

The story we got was that the Arab wanted the Flyers in the package so the franchise could be sold to a New York venture group to possibly relocate it in Baltimore, the city chosen as first alternate by the NHL if any of the six selected expansion cities defaulted.

Other equity holders complied, but Snider balked, as did Wolman's friend, partner and lawyer, Earl Foreman, who was married to Ed's older sister, Phyllis. Earl sided with Snider in the dispute and the battle lines were drawn.

Wolman was shocked that Foreman, his longtime ally, didn't back him.

"Jerry," Earl shrugged, "Eddie's my brother-in-law."

I've got to say a few words here about Earl Marin Foreman, who wasn't readily known in Philly, but was a giant in Washington legal circles and a brilliant sportsman who held ownerships in the NBA Baltimore Bullets, ABA Virginia Squires (who drafted Julius Erving), the Eagles, the Flyers and the Spectrum, founded the Major Indoor Soccer League and owned the Washington Whips soccer team.

Earl was a warm, charming guy who would sit next to Wolman or Snider at crucial negotiations and whisper sage, calming advice when things got heated. He was ruddily handsome, with a cherubic, dimpled face, an easy smile, floppy hair and eyebrows that arched mischievously.

He was a pragmatic strategist who helped arrange the 1970 merger of the NFL and American Football League as well as the merger of the 1976 NBA and American Basketball Association, in which the NBA admitted the more successful franchises of the Denver Nuggets, New York Nets, Indiana Pacers and San Antonio Spurs.

He was an Army medic in Europe in World War II and even had a stint as an FBI lawyer. Pretty decent credentials, I'd say.

This alleged Arab deal made no sense to us. We believed the Flyers conditional franchise legally could not be sold or transferred. Who was this group? Who were these Arabs? Middle East brokers for some oil zillionaire? Scam artists? The whole shmegeggy smelled of sweat and desperation.

Snider offered to buy his share of the Flyers from Wolman, but said Jerry insisted the hockey franchise had to be included. Eventually, Snider and Foreman exchanged their interests in the building for Wolman's shares of the hockey team and Snider became the majority owner of the team.

As early as 1964, Snider had become disillusioned when Wolman shockingly gave much-maligned Eagles coach Joe Kuharich a 15-year, $1-million contract and added the title of general manager.

It was perceived by the press as spiteful and a smack in the face to fans and critics of Kuharich, some of whom hired a plane to fly a "Joe Must Go" banner over Franklin Field during Eagles games.

"That hiring was idiotic," Snider later said. "He did it on a whim and told no one."

Wolman said the nearly completed arena could stand on its own without a hockey team, something that Ed and I felt would work about as well as the sinking Hancock Building. Today, that might work, but in 1967 the big city arena concert business was nowhere. In fact, in its first five years the Spectrum averaged only about four concerts per year.

A few arenas actually exist today solely as music venues, with a few other events thrown in. The Los Angeles Forum, which opened in 1967 as home to the NBA Lakers and NHL Kings, thrives without either team. Both teams moved in 1999, along with the WNBA Sparks, to the Staples Center, about ten miles away in downtown Los Angeles. The Forum, with 17,500 seats and acres of parking, is smaller and cozier than today's venues of over 20,000.

How sad is it that the Spectrum, with its renowned concert sound, international rep and millions of fervent fans, couldn't have been transformed into a music mecca?

The Arab deal and a power grab by Kuharich was the end as far as Snider was concerned. And things got ugly.

Wolman called him disloyal and fired him from the Eagles on October 19, 1967, the day of the first Flyers home game at the Spectrum.

"Betray him? Hell, I was being loyal to our new employees and to the city," Snider told me a couple nights later at dinner. "I wasn't about to just dump everybody *and* see Philadelphia lose the franchise."

I admired both Jerry Wolman and Ed Snider, and it saddened me to see what went down between these ideal opposites: Jerry, the boyish, charismatic visionary, and Ed, the focused, driven businessman.

Through it all, I stayed friends with both, working with Ed every day, even writing a $1,000 check to a fund to help save Jerry's Eagles. Jerry returned it, saying he appreciated it, but it wouldn't help. "Like spit in the ocean," he said about helping his foundering $100-million empire. Wolman at first was unaware of the fund, started by friends in his hometown of Shenandoah, and insisted it be closed and all donations returned. "I couldn't accept money from people who couldn't really afford it," he said.

In early 1969, Jerry told me he knew he had to sell the Eagles. "I put you in for $25,000," he confided, "for being a mensch." A few months later, on May 1, with debts of over $85 million and nowhere to turn, creditors forced him to sell the team to trucking heir Leonard Tose for $16,155,000. After the banks and some 300 other creditors grabbed theirs, Wolman walked away from the table pretty much broke.

Ironically, 16 years later, the high-living Tose was forced to sell the Eagles to auto dealer Norman Braman to satisfy more than $25 million in casino debts. After paying off all his creditors from the $65 million sale, Tose, an admitted gambling addict and alcoholic—who once lost $5 million on a single roll of dice at Harrah's Casino in Atlantic City—frittered away his proceeds with continued lavish living and in 2003, at age 88, died penniless. Former Eagles coach Dick Vermiel, ex-GM Jim Murray and others helped cover the rent for his room at the Warwick Hotel in center city Philadelphia to the end.

Snider owned 7 percent of the Eagles and Earl Foreman had 20 percent. Both cashed out handsomely.

My 25K? Never saw a dime.

"Typical Wolman good-guy bullshit," Snider said.

I met Ed, Earl and a few others at Lou Mayo's a few hours after the settlement, as they were celebrating their windfalls over a late supper. The jubilance bothered me. I quietly left the table after a while and impulsively reached in my pocket, paid off their tabs and headed out to 30th and Market.

I arrived around midnight, just in time to hug Jerry wordlessly as he departed the Eagles offices for the very last time. Neither of us were dry eyed.

He paused on the sidewalk, drained and beaten, took a final drag on his Lucky Strike and like the movies' Humphrey Bogart, flicked it into the street.

He looked back with a sad smile, slid into a waiting car and vanished.

From that point, Wolman and Snider's fortunes veered in vastly different directions: Ed, ultimately building one, and Jerry, unable to rekindle his.

Jerry did make a score or two in real estate, but an attempt to buy back the Eagles fell through in court with Tose denying he had ever offered such an arrangement.

Nearly 40 years later, in 2009, the *Daily News*' Stan Hochman interviewed Wolman and Snider as the Spectrum neared demolition.

Hochman quoted Wolman: "I took him out of the gutter and he [fucked] me!"

Was Wolman invited to the demolition? "Only if he's inside the building," snapped Snider.

"Grumpy old men," Hochman called the two of them.

Wolman castigated Snider in his book. Ed wanted to strike back and asked me to underline any reference for his lawyers to consider. I did, but cautioned Ed not to fire back because it would lead to Wolman's book getting more publicity and prolonging the issue. He said he didn't care. He was being hounded by the media for a response to Wolman's charges.

"Ed," I finally advised, "Here's your only response," and handed him a statement I had just written:

Jerry Wolman and I worked very closely together many years ago, and at one time enjoyed a good relationship. Unfortunately, in many partnerships, things don't always work out and people move on. And that's what happened with Jerry and me. I've moved on and am not interested in rehashing events that may or may not have occurred more than four decades ago. I'm very proud to be spending my time and energy these days running a company that has created thousands and thousands of jobs and has brought happiness and excitement to millions of fans and to be engaged in charitable and civic causes that benefit the community.

He went solely with that statement, and things quieted down.

The feud simmered until Wolman, again pretty much broke, died in 2013 at age 86. Ed passed away in 2016 at age 83, with Earl following nine months later at age 92.

To the end, Wolman had felt Snider was a traitor. Snider said Wolman bailed, and the Flyers and Spectrum wouldn't have happened if he hadn't picked up the pieces. Over time, Wolman made his peace with Earl Foreman. But Ed would have none of it, and never got over Wolman publicly dumping him.

"The sonuvabitch fired me on the Flyers' opening day," he said. "I was egotistically destroyed."

I lived through the whole mess and saw the toll it took on these memorable men.

They're gone now—and who's to say who's right and wrong?

Maybe it's time to put it to rest.

7

The Golden Ticket
Box Office Shenanigans

This has nothing to do with *Willy Wonka and the Chocolate Factory*, except mostly everybody knows the term "golden ticket" from the movie. Having a "golden ticket" meant you won something incredibly valuable, magical even. For many locals, maybe most, getting to see the Eagles finally win the Super Bowl in 2017, or having seen Sinatra, Wilt, Elvis, the Beatles or Air Jordan in person was like having a golden ticket.

What we in the arena business know is that the tickets are literally gold. If I walked into the Spectrum box office and spotted a ticket on the floor under the counter, I told the rookie ticket seller, "That's a fifty-dollar bill lying there. Pick it up!" Or when I could see a scam going on, that was real money being stolen, not just tickets, or ducats or pasteboards as we also called them. So tickets, golden or otherwise, are what get you in to see the magic. They're how the building and the promoter get paid and how they know the count is correct.

There were exceptions. As I wrote earlier, Colonel Parker, who ran Elvis's career, would send in a crew a few weeks before his show and then again the day-of and they would physically count—and I mean physically touch every seat in the house—and that's how the Colonel knew how much he was to take away at the end of the night.

The morning after one Elvis show, Colonel Parker stopped in my office to chat and invited me to fly back to Las Vegas with him and Elvis. "There's plenty of room, and Elvis usually takes a pill and sleeps," he said. "He's fussy about who goes on the plane, but he said you were cool."

Wait, Elvis thinks *I'm* cool? Wow! I want that on my tombstone.

But stupid me had a stupid meeting the next day and I had to decline the tempting, once in a blue suede moon, offer. Been kicking myself over that *forever!*

At any place I ever worked, and I guess everywhere even now, the box office (or B.O.) is what makes you or breaks you. This means that you are always careful whom you put in there.

With union ticket sellers, for us it meant that you were getting people who knew their business, for which we had to pay a premium. But this could also include monkey business, so you always had somebody you really trusted watching every move.

The same went with the ticket takers because they could be running their own game, either with somebody in the box office or on the outside. In the old days, before electronic scanners, ticket takers ripped the ticket and dropped the end of it, or the stub (hence, StubHub) into a secure metal bin atop the turnstile which was called "the drop."

We always had somebody watching the doors, and collected the drops about halfway into an event and locked them up for the night in the box office. The following morning, trusted staffers would count the stubs by hand and compare them to the numbers registered on the turnstiles. If you had more than one percent difference (190 extra turnstile spins without stubs on a crowd of 19,000) you knew there probably was hanky-panky going on.

My first job in the ticket end of the business was as an usher at the old Arena in Philly, where I learned that there was money to be made by upgrading patrons into better seats, which I wasn't comfortable doing. But I never ratted on anybody about it either.

Then one day, in the time before the union came in, I was told that I would be turning in my usher's jacket for a ticket taker's garb. This was a big deal for me. I used to slip in the fire door as a kid, so I took my new role seriously. So did my bosses, who had an ex-cop named Dennis Franks watch us like a hawk, coming over two or three times a night to make sure I hadn't moved the turnstile to let somebody slip by, or maybe I had a cohort outside or in the box office and would split the take.

I learned pretty early that whenever there was people and money, there were tricks and scams.

At the Spectrum, one of the biggest rip-offs was in the early seventies when security found a conspiracy between door staffers and their partners-in-crime out in the parking lot. Mr. Outside would collect ten bucks, give his "customer" an unlit cigarette to carry cupped in hand and say what door to go in. Mr. Inside would see the signal and let the guy in. The signal was changed every day, and the cash collected by Mr. Outside would be whacked up later with the ticket taker.

I also learned that crooks would buy tickets, report them as stolen, then sell the replacements in the parking lot. Others used sophisticated printers at their offices to make fake tickets. One night, at a Rolling Stones concert, we had five people show up for the same seat. The person with the legit ticket was seated and the others, shown the door.

What I tell people now is to use the venue's box office, online or otherwise, as the safest way to a seat, or if not, then use legitimate ticket-selling businesses such as StubHub, eBay, and so on that offer some consumer protection.

There were many ways to get good tickets back then, even for sellouts. Paying an established ticket broker several bucks over the ticket price was one safe way. Scanning the want ads in the local papers, especially the alt weeklies, was a risk, but usually okay. Sometimes, sex was used to get tickets. There were groupies who gladly traded a hand job, oral sex or even a quickie in a car outside the building for good tix or a coveted backstage pass.

The further I climbed the ladder in the business, the more dramatic and bizarre the experiences became. One winter afternoon as I returned in my car from lunch, an attractive brunette maybe pushing 40 approached as I pulled into my spot in front of the Spectrum. Several feet away stood two teenage girls. I rolled my window down and she leaned in, with a big smile on her face. I couldn't help but see her coat was open, revealing some serious cleavage.

"Is there any way," she winked, "that we can get all access passes for my daughters to meet David Cassidy tonight?"

Back then, Cassidy was a teeny-bopper idol who drew 15,000 girls in training bras, like Justin Bieber or Taylor Swift today. "Sorry," I said, "I can't do that," and handed her two Cassidy tee shirts from a pile I had sitting on the passenger side seat.

"Are you sure?" she asked, eyeing my tailored suit and silk tie. "You look like you could arrange anything."

"Sorry," I said once again. "Why don't you just give these shirts to your girls?"

"You don't know what you're missing," she purred, bright red lipstick framing the words, and sashayed back to her kids.

I missed out on a lot of things that my position offered up, but I couldn't let something like that get around. Funny thing is, I had a firm rule about backstage passes. I never asked a promoter for a pass for my own kids for a show. That's just how I played it.

Another time, I got a call from "Downtown." In Philly, "Downtown" means South Philly, which has been known to harbor certain people you don't want to mess with. The call was on behalf of a mob guy whose name I immediately recognized. "My boss would like for you to come for a visit," he said politely. I can't say no even though I know it's going to be a conversation that I don't want to have.

Later that day I get to this little store-front, coffee shop/social club on Passyunk Avenue, and the boss, whose street name is "The Butcher," is sitting in the back like in the movies. He's sipping an espresso out of a demitasse cup with his pinkie out and he tells me to have one, and maybe I want some cake or something. "Cheesecake," he tells a beefy guy lurking nearby. "New York cheesecake—for Lou the Jew," he laughs. I take no offense at this. It was maybe the millionth time I had that flung my way, usually good-naturedly, as in this case—I hoped.

There's a weasel-faced guy sitting next to him with a gold chain and cross covering half of his wife-beater who doesn't say a word, and when my host gives him the nod, he takes out a wad of bills that could choke a hog—before it's butchered.

"My daughter wants to take my twin granddaughters to see the circus Sunday," he says, and the flunky peels off ten $100 bills. "Good seats," he says, "four on the first row maybe—and they'd like to get there early and get photos with that lion tamer and some clowns." His eight-year-old granddaughters, he explains, have posters of hunky Gunther Gebel-Williams and of Ringling Bros. and Barnum & Bailey Circus clowns all over their bedroom. Cute, I think, they'll probably run off and join the circus someday, shacked up with hairy Armenian tumblers.

Huh? Is that it? Can't be that simple. This guy was a Capo, a made mob member who reported directly to Philly's crime boss, Angelo Bruno.

I say, "Sure, no problem." I finish my espresso, while they sit there expressionless, ready to lay more "requests" on me.

And the Capo says, "I'd also like to call you if there's a nice show. None of that jigaboo shit. Something for the family, like the Ice Capades, Peggy Fleming. Maybe Frank or Barbra when they come, shows like that."

I mentioned earlier that Bruno controlled the vending machine business in Philly and from Atlantic City to Trenton. My folks had one of his spring-loaded, hand-cranked five-cent slot machines, about the size of a box of Scott tissues, along with a ten-cent punch board, both out of sight at the end of the counter at our store. If three cherries came up on the slot machine, it would spit out three nickels. If one of the tiny, accordioned pieces of paper that a player popped from any sealed hole on the punch board with a slim metal stylus had a figure on it—from ten cents to one dollar—the customer would get paid in cash from my mom or dad, less ten cents per the number of punched paper slips sitting on the counter.

Our week's take, less the payouts, averaged about 10 bucks net, which was split with the "friendly" guy who came around every Friday afternoon promptly at 4:00 to collect and sell us a new punch board for two bucks. Our store grossed about $75 a day with a net of around 15 percent, or about $12, so an additional five bucks' profit on the illegal activities was manna from heaven. On occasion, a cop or detective would stroll in, ostensibly looking through some cheesy magazines before getting around to eyeing Bruno's equipment. My folks would hand them a couple packs of Lucky Strike or Chesterfield cigarettes, which sold for 25 cents in the 1950s. They'd nod and leave, sometimes grabbing a ten-cent girlie magazine, called *Bachelor* or *Rogue*, on the way out. Expensive magazines like *Playboy*, which cost a half buck, were kept behind the counter.

Bruno was a respected elder who kept things nice and peaceful for over twenty years. That is, until 1980, when some young guns, anxious to move the crime family into the newly lucrative drug biz, put a shotgun against the back of his head and blew him away.

The assassination as Bruno sat in his car in front of his house at 10th Street and Snyder Avenue triggered a years-long bloody war as Philly hoods fought each other for control, while also battling New York's Gambino mob, which decided to muscle its way back into Atlantic City now that casinos were approved.

"I'll take care of the circus tickets," I tell "the Butcher," anxious to get the hell out of there.

"Oh, and by the way," he says, as I rise from the table, "If I should send you a couple of fine neighborhood boys looking for work, maybe you could take care of them, you know?"

"No problem," I tell him, figuring I could put them somewhere where we could watch them closely, maybe on the night changeover crew made up mostly of moonlighting sailors from the nearby Navy Yard and supervised by a Navy captain as straight and tough as they come.

I thank him for the espresso "and Jew cake," which gets a raucous laugh, and leave, glad not to be in some criminal conspiracy—or worse.

I take the thousand bucks to the box office and inform the manager to set up an account for "the gentleman." He is to be sent a receipt showing he has a future credit in tickets of $955, after deducting four front-row circus tickets at $10 plus $5 for VIP parking. It is important to send a message that I will help him out, but not be "owned."

I called Ed Snider to fill him in, as he had been as apprehensive about "the meet" as I was.

"How'd it go?" he said.

"No problem," I said.

"No trouble?"

"No, just access to some tickets and ..."

"I don't want to know," he said and hung up.

When the Spectrum opened, there were only a handful of ticket brokers in the city—wizened, cigar-smoking old-timers—who had been in business for years, eking it out with local pre-Broadway try-outs at the Forrest and Walnut Street Theaters; with club acts like Lenny Bruce, Don Rickles, Mort Sahl, Shelley Berman, Johnny Mathis, Joey Bishop or Jackie Mason at the Latin Casino on Walnut Street or at Tiger Lil Reis' Celebrity Room; and big entertainers like Sinatra, Sammy Davis Jr. and the Will Mastin Trio or Dean Martin and Jerry Lewis at Skinny D'Amato's 500 Club in Atlantic City.

Eagles tickets against the Redskins and Giants were in demand as were big fights involving Philly boxers like middleweight champ Joey Giardello, light-heavyweight champ Harold Johnson or heavyweight king Jersey Joe Walcott. Then there were corporate clients who needed good seats at the last minute, especially to New York City Broadway shows and Yankees games. In those days, the Philly area housed numerous national headquarters like Sunoco, Atlantic Refining, Stetson Hats, Cigna, Pennsylvania Railroad, Budd Company, RCA, DuPont and Philco. After the Flyers and 76ers took off, the number of brokers grew to about ten.

They were a demanding, competitive bunch, always wanting the best seats to the biggest shows and trying to avoid buying in advance so they wouldn't be "stuck with inventory." Some tried to bribe staffers in the box office by paying "ice"—a fee per ticket—to have my people in their hip pocket. Any time I found one of my staffers on their payroll, I fired them on the spot. But human nature being human nature, employees sometimes would succumb to the easy money of holding back the best tickets from the public and selling them to the brokers.

I squeezed the brokers hard, cutting them off. Then they started "sending in the clowns," those who would wait in line overnight to get the best tickets as soon as a show went on sale. We countered that by wrist-banding the first 50 or 100 people in line to buy tickets by lottery.

Eventually, the brokers formed an association and came in to negotiate. I settled things by treating all of them equally, allowing each to purchase up to 20 "good" tickets to every event, not just cherry-pick the hot-ticket shows, with a right to return unsold ducats no later than 48 hours before the event. It helped them have a good supply and it helped the building move a lot of tickets.

At one point, one of the biggest brokers, Oscar, a wonderful Damon Runyan character who boasted he could obtain "seats anywhere in the world," fell out of favor with Electric Factory Concerts, the region's powerful concert promoters, and he came to me with an offer I had to refuse.

"The motherfuckers won't talk to me," he says, "They send back my gifts, the little bastards. Make me a meeting and you get five big ones [$5,000]. Make a marriage, you get fifteen."

I listen, because Oscar is such a likeable character, straight out of Central Casting, cussing and spit-spraying. I can't help but love the guy. I tell him I'll see what I can do, but let him know straight away that his money doesn't interest me.

Some time goes by and, with a few urges from me and others, Oscar the broker and the promoters kiss and make up. He calls me and says he wants to thank me. We meet for lunch at Bain's Deli on Broad Street, a popular lunch joint that has a giant plaster of Paris cheesecake in the window and features "home-made" hot food, which wasn't made in any home I'd ever been in.

I took a bite of my juicy pastrami on rye.

"Here," he says, pushing a fat manila envelope across the table. "I got something for your birthday."

I push it back. He shoves it across to me.

"Sorry, Oscar, I already get paid to do stuff like this," I said, pushing it back.

"Are you crazy?" he sputters, as minced bits of corned beef, sour kraut and Russian dressing foul the air. "Nobody turns down money!"

I gave him the "Lou the Jew" look.

"I do," I said, dropped a five-dollar bill on the table for my lunch and walked out. One more guy who couldn't say he owned me.

Besides, it wasn't even my birthday.

About a year later, I'm with my neighborhood softball team at Palumbo's big nightclub in South Philly, and who comes by the table but Mr. Broker himself. He was happy. And drunk.

"Hey Asshole," he says, smiling, "What are you guys doing here?" I tell him my softball team is celebrating winning the league championship.

"Softball?" he roars. "I'll show you softballs."

With that he moves closer, unzips his fly and unfurls the biggest set of family jewels I'd ever seen.

"For chrissakes," I choke out. "Oscar, put those away!"

Mr. Broker, who goes about 5'8" or 5'9" and weighs over 200 pounds, cleans up his act, leans over and stuffs a roll of bills in my suit pocket. "Hold these for me," he says, shuffling off. "I'm too drunk to have all this cash on me, and you're maybe the most honest cock-sucker I know."

In Oscar-speak, that's a compliment.

Maybe two months go by with no word from him. Then out of the blue one day, he visits my office.

First thing he says: "You got my money?" No "Hello," no "Asshole," nothing. Not even for an honest cocksucker?

I unlock my top left desk drawer and take out the roll of bills. "Six hundred and thirteen dollars," I say, flipping it across my desk toward him, still wrapped in the big rubber band as he had handed it to me.

"It was seven hundred and thirteen dollars, you fuckin' thief!" he yells.

"I know," I reply. "Just wanted to see if you even knew how much you had that night. It's all there."

He laughed until his face turned beet red and I thought he was going to choke. "You cocksucker, you counted it, didn't you?" he said. Not only did I count it at Palumbo's that night, but I had two guys from my softball team, one an assistant district attorney and the other a banker, verify the amount.

By 1970, tickets had gone electronic. Ticketron, a New York company backed by Control Data Corp., was trying to get off the ground, using new computerized event ticketing technology. The company wanted to distribute tickets to arenas, stadiums and theaters over telephone landlines to terminals at remote locations, but couldn't crack the tight New York market. So they contacted me to see if we wanted to help launch it in Philly.

I got them kick-started by putting a large allotment of tickets to every Spectrum event on their system. Ticketron installed terminals in area stores that I selected. This meant foot traffic for our sponsors like Sears, Roebuck & Co. and Strawbridge & Clothier, which could instantly sell tickets at several of their Philly locations.

After some early glitches, more and more of our tickets were sold in advance, especially for hot concerts, with lines of fans snaking through the stores waiting for tickets to be spit out of the electronic box offices. The stores charged a small fee per ticket and meanwhile brought in customers. Ticketron gave us a piece of the fee. Shows sold out. Everyone was happy.

Quickly, other arenas, teams and theaters signed on to Ticketron, and the ticket business changed forever. Remote locations suddenly were everywhere, and so it was until the '90s when the internet blew them out, offering tickets to everything online, and of course even allowing buyers to print them at home.

Now the only hard tickets usually printed are for season ticket subscribers, although some teams don't print them at all, ending an era when fans saved tickets as souvenirs from big memorable events. With everything online, the big-ticket companies find themselves in fierce competition and contentious litigation with artists, teams and buildings that sell tickets on their own networks, allowing them to jack up and keep all fees.

This can add up.

For a pre-pandemic Celine Concert at the Wells Fargo Center in Philadelphia, two lower-level tickets were $245.50 each at the box office. Then there were $92 in fees plus $3.25 to print them at home. Total: $586.25. Add in $30 for parking and $100 for drinks and a snack each, and you got yourself one hell of a deal, emphasis on "hell."

There have been complaints and lawsuits against the ticket companies and arenas for diverting customers to other systems that they own or have an arrangement with for further inflated costs. Even Bruce Springsteen was furious at what he publicly called the "emerging ticket monopoly."

Tickets up to the day that COVID-19 halted the concerts and events were outrageously expensive. Concert-goers didn't mind paying to see their idols in person, but a family of four easily had to shell out over $1000 for tickets, parking, program, popcorn and sodas. They paid it if they could because there weren't many opportunities for a family to share the magic of a big concert, ice skating or a touring Jurassic World Live show unless they settled for cheaper seats in the upper level.

I loved seeing kids' faces at a Spectrum ice show or when the circus used to play. But it bothered me that some of them were sitting so far away. When possible, I moved folks down from the nose-bleed seats and often had hawkers treat them to hot dogs and sodas.

Leaving work one bitter January night shortly before a circus performance, I was sitting a block away at a red light and noticed a Black man and four little kids trudging in the dark toward the Broad Street subway entrance on Pattison Avenue. Some of the kids were crying.

I pulled over and asked if they were ok. The man said he was taking his kids to see the show, but the tickets were more expensive than he expected and he had only enough money to get all but one child in.

"I had some coupons from Acme Markets," he explained, "but they said they weren't good for tonight's show."

This got my blood boiling. I could see they were a poor family, and that the kids were crushed.

"Please," I said, "All of you get in my car."

I took them back to the building and directly up into an available suite. I called catering to arrange food and drinks and told the manager on duty to get clowns to come up at intermission with souvenirs. This was going to be a night they'd never forget.

Then I made a bee line for the box office. The manager on duty said they had been a few dollars short for five tickets. "It's policy," he said. God, was I pissed!

"Well, here's a new policy," I said, angrily enough for the whole box office to hear. "If this ever happens again, you let them in and charge my personal account for the difference. I don't care if it's a few dollars or a hundred. Don't ever do that to a family! Did you see their faces when you turned them away?" I asked. "Would you like that to happen to your kids? Have a fucking heart! And guess what? I want you to go up to their suite and apologize—and, after the show, drive them home!"

He looked at me, stunned.

"Don't worry," I said, "I'll see that you get mileage and overtime for whatever runs over your shift."

He got the message. They all did that night.

This is not to say I'm a softie. I know my business and I know the scams. Hell, we could afford a few freakin' bucks a year to make someone's dream.

But I didn't want to be seen as a sucker. For instance, when we had dance concerts for performers like the Beastie Boys, the tickets were all GA (general admission), which means we couldn't use the number of seats to verify sales. This was an invitation to all kinds of scams.

One night, the fire marshal showed up and complained that the crowd appeared to exceed our legal capacity of 19,500. "There has to be nearly 20,000 people in here," he warned.

I alerted security to be particularly attentive at the next GA event.

At the following dance concert, we hand counted the ticket stubs *during* the show and there were nearly 300 more stubs than tickets reported sold. At the next GA event there were about the same number too many. Security reported spotting some ticket takers keeping entire tickets instead of handing back stubs and slipping them to a runner who rushed out and resold them in the parking lot. After the show, of course, they would divvy up.

We pulled them into an office and got them to talk or be busted.

Three hundred tickets resold at $6 netted a pot of $1,800, or $600 each. Not bad for a night's work—and a lot more than I was making.

They asked for a second chance. I fired them on the spot. They were lucky I didn't call the cops.

They needed to heed the Golden Rule: "It's my gold, don't break the rule."

8

The House That Rock Built

Philly's a Music Mecca

I love music, but don't know a riff from a reefer.

Actually, I do know a reefer. Weed was introduced to me by a young secretary at the Spectrum. She was a flower child. I was a three-piece suit. Certainly, the odd couple. It eased the constant pressure of the job in slow, late afternoon walks around the outside of the building or in the dimness of the last row of the upper deck. It also heightened intimate moments with her to the level of heaven.

Even though I've seen maybe 200 concerts, mostly at the Spectrum, I couldn't tell you the lyrics of any current song.

I love the pounding rock from the Stones to Green Day, but I grew up on ballads: crooners like Sinatra, Perry Como, Eddie Fisher, Vic Damone, Jerry Vale, Peggy Lee, Dinah Shore, Sarah Vaughan, Nat King Cole, Dionne Warwick and Mel Tormé. Songs that you could actually follow—and slow dance to the words.

"I've got you under my skin . . . deep in the heart of me . . ." So deep that those words are still really a part of me.

The concerts I've enjoyed the most, Mick Jagger aside, are the Who, Chicago, the Beach Boys, Prince and Earth, Wind and Fire.

Saw Elvis several times, the last time as a bloated, sweating shadow of the King, who passed away weeks later.

I saw Sinatra at all eleven of his Spectrum appearances, plus years earlier at Philly's Convention Hall with child bride Mia Farrow swooning in the front row. I was too young to see him when he played the Earle Theater on Market Street in the forties, or I would have been there.

Concert nuts probably think I should thank my stars for being able to see all those great bands and performers, literally from A to Z—from the Allman Brothers to ZZ Top. Absolutely, though I was technically on the job and tending to any trouble.

I thought Green Day, with manic Billy Joe Armstrong killing it in the Spectrum's last days of summer 2009, delivered one of the building's best rock shows ever, right up there with the Stones' early shows. Pearl Jam, closing the building with four rousing nights in October 2009, was a smash.

Neil Diamond was a nice guy to hang with and he sells out everywhere but, to me, he was totally cloying on stage. Cher and Madonna needed to drop the mic years ago, but I more recently found Lady Gaga to be a gem.

Don't laugh, but I thought Justin Bieber, that spoiled brat, was really talented—singing, playing guitar, drums, piano and trumpet. Full disclosure, I saw only part of his show several years ago, as I picked up my daughter at the Wells Fargo Center, but was duly impressed.

I was never into rap or calypso, mon, but I loved going to the old small clubs owned by Herb Spivak or Larry Magid to see the jazz of Dave Brubeck and Herbie Mann and the Cuban congas of Mongo Santamaria and many of the doo-wop and soul groups. That was before the Spectrum even opened.

The best all-around Spectrum shows for me were Sinatra, Liza Minelli and Sammy Davis Jr. together in 1988, and thirteen years earlier, Sinatra, Ella Fitzgerald and Count Basie.

I couldn't tell you one song from Katy Perry, Beyoncé, Celine Dion, Rihanna, Mariah Carey or Taylor Swift. I admired the great Aretha, but the diva Patti LaBelle assaults my ears.

I may be tone deaf, but I do know that the Spectrum, America's showplace, truly was "the House That Rock Built."

No band skipped Philadelphia once the Spectrum opened in 1967. Thanks to the genius of Electric Factory Concerts impresarios Herb and Alan Spivak and promoter Larry Magid, it became a must-stop for bands from around the world. You didn't play New York, LA or Chicago without hitting the Spectrum—the Big Four concert towns.

Herb Spivak kicked things off by opening the building on Saturday, September 30 and Sunday, October 1, 1967 with something he called the 2nd Annual Quaker City Jazz Festival, showcasing a who's who of stars.

"I didn't know if it would work or I'd go bust," he told me recently. "Booking a big arena that hadn't even opened yet was a huge risk, but I knew Philly was a great music town and rolled the dice."

We turned him down at first because we didn't think a jazz bill would sell and didn't want to open with a flopperoo. Herb, a business-minded, 30-year-old local music promoter and owner of the popular Showboat jazz club at Broad and Lombard Streets, told us, "That's my problem." So we rolled with him.

Of course, both nights sold out, and the crowds poured in even as seats were still being bolted into place and the as-yet-unpaved dirt parking lot was filling with cars. They backed up so far up Broad Street that we delayed the concert about an hour the first night, finally lighting up the stage with Dizzy Gillespie playing "God Bless America."

With Electric Factory booking jazz and rock and radio personality Georgie Woods and promoter Irv Nahan bringing in the Black acts, the Spectrum prospered. FM radio was taking off too, and it was the right time and place for a big-time concert explosion. It's when rock 'n roll came of age.

It was a different America: Flower Power. Liberation. Drugs. Vietnam protests. The Chicago Seven. Kent State University killings. Counterculture. Race riots. The still fresh assassination of President Kennedy and, later, his brother Robert and Martin Luther King, Jr. The Cuban missile crisis. Nixon. Distrust of government, of people over 30, and of "The Man."

But an arena was a place where people could come together as one in a tribal kind of way. To lose themselves amid the roar of music or fanaticism of sports and get away from it all, if even for just a few hours. This was never more evident than during the COVID-19 lockdowns.

The elite sat with the masses. Black, white, rich or poor, GOP or Dems. We rose as an army to defeat the hated Celtics of Boston and the haughty Rangers of New York and the evil Red Army skaters from Russia.

What made the Spectrum click?

For a room that could hold over 19,000 people, it had an intimacy. The stands were on top of the action and the compactness of the building delivered astounding sound. Acts like Springsteen, Billy Joel and the Dead loved the building. One band after another sounded great and the roaring throngs energized them in return. There was an electricity about it.

"We spent a fortune on sound at the CoreStates Center," recalled Ed Snider, calling it by its original name when the glitzy palace opened across from the Spectrum in 1996. "But not one extra dime on Spectrum sound."

"These old venues build up a certain degree of soul," Bruce told the *Philadelphia Inquirer* before it closed. "They don't make arenas like this anymore. And they ended up being ideal for rock shows—without the luxury boxes," Springsteen said, praising the "democraticness" of the Spectrum. Amazingly, when the Boss opened for Chicago in 1973, it was his first time playing an arena, and it didn't go well. The audience, demanding Chicago, booed!

There was a grittiness about the place, with its tight bathrooms, jam-packed concourse and gummy floors. It wasn't unusual to see women skipping those long lines and marching into the men's rooms.

We had a footprint of only four and a half acres of city land on which to build, which turned out to be a blessing. The building was big, but squat and tight.

Acts at first plugged into the arena's basic public address system, then began bringing in their own amps, becoming more elaborate every year. Seats were smaller (as were fannies) and leg room tight, but who cared—who sat? Arenas now must have a minimum 33 inches of "tread width" between rows. The Spectrum had a toe-pinching 30.

Larry Magid came up with "Dance Concerts," meaning no seats on the hockey rink–sized floor. Not only could we sell more tickets this way, but people could move around—and actually dance.

More than 1,000 acts graced the Spectrum with over 2,300 concerts in its 42 years, solidifying Philly's rep as one of the nation's most thriving musical centers.

"Other buildings were afraid of bringing in certain acts," said Magid. "Like Alice Cooper and his guillotine or Black Sabbath's Ozzy Osbourne (reportedly) biting off the head of a bat. But Ed Snider and the Spectrum kept an open mind. This place took risks, actively supported the concert business and in many ways allowed us to innovate."

The Grateful Dead played the Spectrum 53 times; Yes, 27 times; Billy Joel, 25; Aerosmith, 22; Jethro Tull, Rod Stewart and Van Halen, 19 each; Neil Diamond and Elton John, 18; Rush, 17; the Beach Boys, Chicago, Country Joe and the Fish and Luther Vandross, 16; Allman

Brothers and Eric Clapton, 15; AC/DC, Black Sabbath and Genesis, 13; Bon Jovi, David Bowie and the Eagles, 12; the Kinks, Frank Sinatra and ZZ Top, 11; Earth, Wind & Fire, the Moody Blues, Ozzy Osbourne, the J. Geils Band, Tom Petty and the Heartbreakers and Bob Seger and the Silver Bullet Band, 10. And the beat goes on.

"We started looking at the Spectrum as really just a big club," said Magid. "What if we didn't have seats on the floor? We said, we'll call them dance concerts. We'll keep the ticket prices low and try to build exciting shows, rather than waiting for the headliners or the Johnny Cashes or the Ray Charleses of the world, which was the standard. Let's break out of this mold, and let's go into the Spectrum with rock shows."

Frank Rizzo was still police commissioner in May 1970 and didn't want the Doors to play Philadelphia because Jim Morrison allegedly had exposed himself at a concert somewhere. So the fire marshal conveniently showed up and said we were in violation because too many people had jammed toward the stage. This wasn't a dance concert. Everyone had a ticket for a seat on the floor.

The crowd paid no attention to the Doors' manager when he asked them to move back. "I was young, and my hair was long," recalled Magid. So he went on stage and made his legendary appeal to the fans, which the Doors recorded as "Announcer 'Sit Down," from *The Doors Live in Philadelphia '70.*

"Last week, we had 25,000 hippies out in the park, man," Magid began, likely referring to America's first Earth Day. "It was beautiful. Now, we want everything to be cool here. We want to do more concerts, but man, there's a couple of small rules. You're just gonna have to move back. Sit down, man, and make aisles. We're not tryin' to bullshit you, man, we're trying to lay it right on the fucking line, man."

The crowd heeded him, and the show went on.

"A lot of it becomes a blur," Magid told *Philadelphia Magazine* in 2009, "because there were so many [shows]. Dylan coming back and playing with the Band, that was a big deal. The Rolling Stones in '69. Elvis in '71. We did a [multi-band] show with Led Zeppelin, and they said 'Jimmy Page is sick. If we don't get him on now, we're not going to be able to do the show.'"

"Unbeknownst to me, all they wanted to do was go to New York and go to some club and party. We had to convince Jethro Tull 'You've got to go on after them.' So Led Zeppelin opened the show and left."

"Springsteen's first show there—he opened for Chicago and got booed, "said Magid. "I remember standing there as he was walking offstage with his head down, and I said, 'This wasn't your night. Nah, this wasn't the show you should have played on.' And he just looked at me. He didn't know me. I said, 'You'll get 'em.' I was just trying to make the guy feel good. I didn't know he was going to be what he's become."

Jon Bon Jovi remembered coming to the Spectrum often because Philly was more accessible from his home in New Jersey than New York.

"I saw Van Halen there," he said. "I saw Bruce at the Spectrum before I saw him at the Garden. It was the spring of 1978. The house lights went down, and I started sweating. I was 15, stage right, lower bowl. I remember it like it was yesterday. They didn't sell it out, not even close. He went up to the top tier, and the seats were empty. He sang 'Spirit in the Night' from up there, and I just said, "That's it. That's what I want to do in life."

Also, longtime WMMR deejay Pierre Robert quoted Bono saying, "We're used to playing smaller venues. This is our first tour of the bigger places. It's so weird to be playing in these airplane hangars." Pierre added: "When the Dead played their 50th show there, I raised a tie-dye banner and did a little speech. The banner was promptly stolen. Some little stoner out there has the Dead 50th-anniversary banner in his room somewhere."

I didn't realize it back then, but the concerts were every bit as important to the success of the Spectrum as the Flyers and 76ers. Magid and the Spivaks—Herb, Allen and, earlier, their brother Jerry—didn't get enough credit for what they brought to the table. Yeah, they made a lot of dough and hit the lottery by selling out to cash-rich Live Nation, but they more than earned it. The Spivaks retired but Magid stayed on, promoting shows with Allen's son, Adam. Prior to the pandemic of 2020, Magid was busy promoting as he neared age 80.

You could say that the expansion of the NHL in 1967 created a string of new venues in which the rock business was born and raised. But it was the innovation and fearlessness of promoters like Electric Factory in Philadelphia and others in Boston, L.A. and Chicago that kept the turnstiles spinning on otherwise dark nights.

Nearly twenty thousand people at an indoor concert was a pulsating celebration, a happening, a coming together of people sharing a night they talk about forever.

"It didn't matter if it was music or anything else in the building—it was the times," added Magid in the *Philadelphia Magazine* interview. "It was political. You wanted to have something sweep you up. We had an unpopular war, an unpopular president. We had rallying points, and people wanted change. It was the birth of popular culture. An event is only so much—the rest is social.

"You hear that song on the radio," Magid said, "and you go back to that moment because there's a great memory there. It was about being at the right place at the right time.

"And that place was the Spectrum."

Courtesy of the author

Courtesy of the author

Left: Celebrating July 4th, 1938 outside my parents' store at age 3.
Right: My dad, Alexander, in front of our store, January 1942.

Courtesy of the author

My Mom, Frances (*right*), with two of her five sisters,
my sister, Suzanne, and bratty me at bottom.

Left: "Front Page Lou" on the lookout for a good story at City Hall newsroom, 1964.

Right: Love this poster presented by our advertising agency in 1972 when I was named arena president.

That's me (*second from left*), between Joe Kadlec and Ed Snider at the Flyers' 1970 NHL Draft in Montreal, the year we got lucky selecting future stars Bill Clement and Bob Kelly.

Left: Explaining why we needed a third deck on Spectrum to Flyers owners (*from left*) Ed Snider, Joe Scott and Fitz Dixon. ['72]

Right: Signing "Boy Wonder" J Russell Peltz to a contract as Spectrum Boxing Director in 1974.

I jokingly describe this as advising Billy Jean King how to handle Bobby Riggs in the famous 1973 Battle of the Sexes match.

Courtesy of the author

Courtesy of the author

Left: Hanging with Flyers GM Keith Allen and Evel Knievel before he zoomed over a line of cars at the Spectrum on his motorcycle in 1971.

Right: "You can thank this guy for getting me here," Kate Smith tells Ed's first wife, Myrna Snider, at the Spectrum in 1973.

Courtesy of the author

Philly Mayor Frank Rizzo was a polarizing figure but helped pave the way for the Spectrum's success. City Hall, 1975.

At my spot in the Super Box for more than 800 Flyers games.

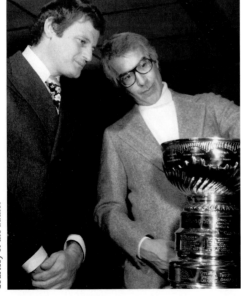

Looking for our names etched on the Stanley Cup after Flyers 1974 season, our first win.

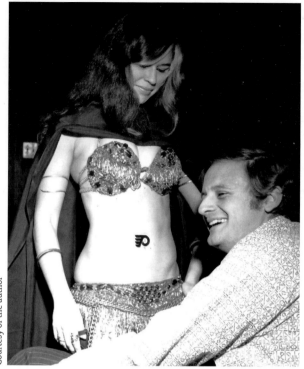

Checking out my surprise "gift" at the Spectrum on my 37th birthday, Nov. 25, 1972.

On the beach at Acapulco with first wives, Myra, and Myrna Snider, 1972.

Waiting anxiously with Ed Snider to see if PRISM network officially launches, 1976.

Pushing the button to officially turn on PRISM, September 1, 1976.

Left: A lone chair in the Spectrum parking lot is a sad reminder of its imminent demise in 2009.

Right: The Spectrum is a wreck! 2010.

The original, 1966, hand-drawn Spectrum rendering still hangs in my office.

9

Rizzo and the Rolling Stones

Gimme Shelter!

The Stones are coming, and people are running for shelter!

The Rolling Stones' historic 1972 tour of North America, with 48 shows in 54 days, was marred by violence at nearly every stop, with riot cops using tear gas and batons to control unruly, often ticketless fans trying to storm the doors.

Two sold-out Spectrum shows were coming up on July 20 and 21, and that spelled trouble with a capital "T." Hot nights in the city! And not from global warming. We knew we had to have our ass in gear, prepped and ready for anything.

The Rolling Stones' first appearance at the Spectrum had been almost three years earlier, on November 25, 1969, my 34th birthday. It was probably the greatest concert I ever saw.

Here's the setlist from that concert:

Jumpin' Jack Flash	Midnight Rambler
Carol	Live with Me
Sympathy for the Devil	Little Queenie
Stray Cat Blues	Satisfaction
Love in Vain	Honky Tonk Woman
Prodigal Son	Street Fighting Man
You Gotta Move	Gimme Shelter
Under My Thumb	

I lost hearing in both ears for nearly two days and never fully got it back in my right one. My box was way too close to the tower of blasting amps, but I still say it was worth it.

We had a few incidents that night, but it was a breeze compared to the pandemonium 11 days later when the bad-boy band rolled into California, creating one of rock's most infamous pop culture legends.

The 1969 Altamont Speedway Free Festival in Northern California was billed as the Woodstock of the West. Headlined and organized in part by the Stones, it also featured, in order of appearance: Santana, Jefferson Airplane, the Flying Burrito Brothers and Crosby, Stills, Nash & Young, with the Stones taking the stage as the final act.

The Grateful Dead also were scheduled to perform but bailed while backstage due to the violence. "That's the way things went at Altamont—so badly that the Grateful Dead, prime organizers and movers of the festival, didn't even get to play," *Rolling Stone* magazine reported.

About 300,000 people packed the grounds. Filmmakers Albert and David Maysles shot considerable footage of the event and incorporated it into the celebrated 1970 documentary film *Gimme Shelter.*

The Stones foolishly hired the feared Hell's Angels biker gang to "police" the crowd near the stage, and it was a disaster. Jagger later would carry a revolver on the tour following alleged biker threats. In a later interview, Mick agreed that hiring the bikers "was a bit naïve." Ya think?

The violence included one stabbing death (by Hell's Angels' stage security) and three other deaths—two by a hit-and-run car and one by drowning in a drainage ditch. At least four births were reported.

The Rolling Stones American Tour 1972, often referred to as the S.T.P. Tour (for Stones Touring Party), was a fabled rock 'n roll happening, although really not more civilized than the first one. It kicked off June 3 and ended July 26, following the May 12 release of their album *Exile on Main St.* It was viewed as an international spectacle, led by the swaggering, preening Mick Jagger, who by then was a bona fide jet-set celeb.

Press coverage was worldwide, with some of the most famous writers, including acclaimed author Truman Capote, chronicling its wicked excesses. Trouble predictably followed the tour, starting with the first show in Vancouver, where 31 policemen were hurt when more than 2,000 fans attempted to storm the Pacific Coliseum.

Ten days later in San Diego, 15 fans were injured and 60, busted. At the Tucson, Arizona show on June 14, police had to use tear gas to quell a mob of 300 youths crashing the gates. Things got more frenzied in Chicago, where the partying group hunkered down in Hugh Hefner's lurid Playboy Mansion instead of a hotel. One writer described it as "a four-day orgy interrupted by the occasional performance." More fireworks happened in Washington, DC on July 4 with 61 arrests at RFK Stadium. Nine days later, Detroit cops repelled 2,000 fans rushing the doors without tickets.

Moving on to Montreal on July 17, things got worse. A bomb destroyed the Stones' equipment van and new gear had to be flown in. As if this wasn't bad enough, 3,000 fake tickets flooded the market, triggering a riot and delaying the concert.

The next day, only two short days before coming to Philadelphia, Jagger and the Stones' Keith Richards were jailed in Boston for fighting with a photographer. Afraid of dire consequences if that night's show at the Boston Garden were cancelled, Beantown Mayor Kevin White ordered them released—in time for another late start to the show.

Philly, here they come!

Fearing the worst, we flooded parking lot encampments days ahead of time with arena uniformed and undercover security, set up cold water stations and extra portable toilets and generally made nice with the milling hippies, junkies and Vietnam protesters. Hot nights in the city for sure. Pot clouds hung heavy in the air, but the cannabis being consumed served to keep things mellow.

We asked the city for extra police, and nightstick law-and-order Mayor Frank Rizzo was only too happy to oblige. He sent down busloads of cops to control the great unwashed.

We had already removed rocks and any other possible projectiles from the flower bed in front of the building and made sure to get all the doors open as soon as the Stones got satisfaction from their sound checks. The Spectrum had huge plate glass windows that cost $2,000 each to replace ($12,000 in today's money). We weren't going to give anyone ammunition.

We set up police horse barriers in a serpentine fashion to limit the crowd from rushing the doors straight on.

We were either very smart or totally lucky—maybe a little of both—on these two steamy nights. There were precious few incidents as the packed crowds exulted while the Stones shared the stage with a rising Stevie Wonder and R&B singer Martha Reeves. We dodged the bullet—or, in this case, a large cannon ball.

An interesting side note was that the Stones' manager asked for the payout to be split, something like $200,000 in a check and $80,000 in cash for the Mick. "We didn't ask any questions," promoter Herb

Spivak told me recently. "It was their money, but I always wondered what he did with all that cash." That's like carrying around a half million bucks today.

With the Stones juggernaut thankfully out of town and on to Pittsburgh—and a nice payday for Electric City Concerts and for the Spectrum—we popped some confiscated champagne and decompressed.

■ ■ ■

But the euphoria didn't last long. It ended abruptly two days later when the mailman delivered something that shook us to the core. It was an invoice from the City of Philadelphia Revenue Department for "police overtime charges" demanding a fee of $63,000. That would be a staggering $400,000 today!

This was the first time we were charged for police services in or outside the building. Normally, city cops took care of street traffic around the building and our security patrolled inside. Cops would get involved inside only if things got out of control like it did six months earlier, on January 6, when all broke loose at a Flyers game. Officers were pummeled as the St. Louis Blues got into a brawl in the stands with fans, then fought the cops. Several Blues players were arrested and jailed overnight and we had to help get them released. Just another night running a big-time arena.

At the time we got the huge bill for the Stones' concert, Ed Snider and attorney Earl Foreman, his brother-in-law, had just taken control of the Spectrum, which had been in Chapter 11 due to the crash of former partner Jerry Wolman. No way could the building afford to pay this huge, unexpected invoice.

Snider literally turned pale when I showed him the bill. He ripped open a fresh pack of Lucky Strikes, the first of four packs he worried through that day.

"Let me call Frank," I calmed Ed, meaning Mayor Rizzo, with whom I had a good relationship. Rizzo, for some reason, didn't like Snider, though he hardly knew him. He felt Snider was "a carpetbagger from DC" who hadn't done much for the city in terms of civic commitment, an area that Snider later contributed to significantly as his organization grew and he became successful.

It wouldn't be the only time that I brokered a deal between these two combative heavyweights that benefited Snider and the arena.

Rizzo was not in the least a sports fan and earlier declined my invitations to attend Spectrum events as our guest. This despite the fact that we had dedicated one of our eight suites to the city as the Mayor's Box.

Snider, who normally feared no man, was nevertheless wary of Rizzo and had a healthy respect for Frank's famous "reward my friends and destroy my enemies" rep. "He scares the shit out of me," Ed confided. "I'm not above groveling if it helps."

I made a few calls, and two days later Ed and I were seated in the mayor's huge, wood-paneled office on the second floor of City Hall.

Big Frank sat behind his mahogany desk, which was the size of an aircraft carrier. Our heavy, immovable guest chairs were at least five feet away from his desk, the top of which was immaculate except for a neat pile of papers and a telephone console with a dozen blinking buttons.

It wasn't the first time I'd been in the mayor's office and it wouldn't be the last. I covered Big Frank's predecessor, Jim Tate, for the *Daily News* and later had audiences with Mayors Ed Rendell and Jim Kenney on other projects. But this was my first visit since Rizzo's close friend, Al Pearlman, a wealthy contractor and staunch supporter, installed $100,000 worth of City Hall renovations for gratis.

The office was festooned with plaques, awards and gifts of sculpture and art from the rich and famous, sports teams and visiting presidents, royalty and the Pope. Frank was coatless, dressed as always in a crisp, white dress shirt with weapon-grade starch and a dark solid blue tie.

Francis Lazarro Rizzo, Sr. was a career cop who began riding with the elite Highway Patrol motorcycle squad, rising quickly to sergeant, captain, police commissioner and mayor. Along the way, he ran roughshod over Blacks and liberals with his tough-cop mentality. He served as mayor for eight years on a law-and-order platform and was nationally known for his salty, colorful, often hurtful comments.

Following President Kennedy's 1961 Bay of Pigs invasion fiasco in Cuba, Rizzo told the nation, "Maybe we should have sent in the Philadelphia police." Promising to handle a particular situation against an enemy, he threatened he'd "make Attila the Hun look like a faggot!" "The streets are safe in Philadelphia," he said in response to a critic. "It's only the people who make them unsafe." And the unforgettable: "A conservative is a liberal who just got mugged."

Rizzo was such a flashpoint for racial protests that a statue erected in his honor, across from City Hall ten years after his 1971 death, was yanked by the city late one night in 2020 after protests by Black Lives Matter activists and vandalizing mobs.

I had met Rizzo years before when he was the swashbuckling police captain of the center city district and I was Front Page Lou, crusading reporter for the *Philadelphia Daily News*. He was keeping a watchful eye on a crowd of young Vietnam war protesters marching and chanting in front of the Bellevue-Stratford Hotel, where Vice President Hubert Humphrey was speaking. I had stopped to say hello to a few detectives who were sources of mine, and they introduced me to The Man.

"Shone-feld!" he bellows, and sticks out a beefy hand for a vigorous shake. My hand disappears into his huge mitt. "Hey men," he yells, "This is the guy who named me 'The Cisco Kid.' I love that!" He piston-pumps my arm, notes that I was younger than he thought and promises that if there's anything I ever need, just to pick up the phone and call him.

Actually another reporter, Joe Daughen, who covered Police HQ, aka "The Round House," bestowed Frank with the colorful moniker following a series of Rizzo police raids on center city clubs and restaurants during which the controversial captain displayed holstered pearl-handled revolvers. But Frank brushed off my protests that it wasn't me who named him, and I didn't push it. Who was I to tell Frank Rizzo he was wrong?

As the years went by, it stood me in good stead with the "Big Bambino," especially after I got to the Spectrum and reached out to his son, Frank Jr., inviting him to games and special events.

I was following the sage advice of little Tony Zecca, the mayor's savvy press secretary, who told me early on not to bother sending Frank Sr. tickets and invites. "Just take good care of 'Frannie' and the Mayor will be in your debt," he advised.

Back in the Mayor's ornate office with Snider, Frank greets me warmly and shoots Ed a cursory nod.

"Mayor," I weigh in. "You never come to the Spectrum to see any games, concerts or family shows. What do you need, a gold-plated invitation?" Frank looks puzzled for a moment. I pull out a Tiffany-ish, blue velvet box the size of a wallet.

"If you do, here it is." I hand it over, Frank opens it and laughs uproariously. A calfskin leather folder, in fact, held a gold-plated, metal lifetime invitation inscribed with his name. That broke the ice and he loosened up.

After a bit of small talk about the city and politics, crime and protests, Frank said, "Well, what brings you gentlemen here today?"

I hand Frank the dreaded $63,000 invoice.

"Oh, that," he says.

He looks it over, fixes his gaze on Snider, tears it in half, again in quarters and flutters it into his waste basket.

"Forget it," he says. "Consider it paid in full."

"I just wanted to see Mr. Snider's ass in my office. Now that I have your attention, Ed," he says looking sternly at Snider, "this goes away."

And so we go away, relieved of debt and the weight of worry.

Outside on the wide plaza surrounding the ornate, 70-year-old City Hall, with its imposing 700 rooms and 12-foot-thick base stone walls, Ed is incredulous.

Shaking his head and eyes wide in disbelief, he fires up a Lucky.

"I can't believe he tore it up—just like that!" he exclaims. "I'd fight anybody, but that guy scares me shitless. Where's the closest fuckin' bar?!"

10

Ol' Blue Eyes and the .38

The Mob Muscles In

The first time I saw Ol' Blue Eyes—The Voice, The Chairman of the Board—was on a grainy, nine-inch Admiral television set at my friend Norman Santora's house.

The show that night caused quite a stir. It was the *Frank Sinatra Timex Show* featuring Ella Fitzgerald. Rocco, Norm's dad, had just turned on the show and settled down in his chair when she came on and sang.

But Mr. Santoro's face became red. "Desgraciales," he said, and then grumbled something about "moolie," which I later learned meant "eggplant" and referred to Ella Fitzgerald. He sat there, his face getting redder and redder, but he wouldn't get up and change the station, as if by touching the television he actually could catch something.

Then he went into the kitchen where Mrs. Santoro was doing the dishes, and Norman and I went back outside and continued our game of half-ball until the streetlights came on, which meant the day was over. I could hear his parents going on about it because you kept your windows open then.

"No good, no good," said Mr. Santoro. "You come from a family like that. What do you expect? She did abortions, Frank's mother did." I imagined Norm's mother crossing herself a dozen times.

That comment ended the discussion because what could you say to that? I read much later that Sinatra's mother, Molly, actually did perform abortions in their little house in Hoboken, New Jersey. "Hatpin Dolly," she was called. His father, Anthony, was an illiterate who quit his job to become a professional fighter, but under the name "Marty O'Brien" because the Irish were getting most of the fights then.

Anthony Sinatra's hands kept breaking and he had to give up the fight game, but he became a captain of the Hoboken Fire Department— it is said without any prior experience—and then opened a successful bar called "Marty O'Brien's."

Frank Sinatra's higher education lasted all of 47 days of high school, but he was equally quick in getting his career "in the business" started. In 1935, at age 19, he was in a group called The Three Flashes, which became the Hoboken Four, and then worked as a singing waiter.

By the time he was 24, he was singing with the Harry James Band and then with Tommy Dorsey. They say that Mr. Dorsey had extracted a contract from Sinatra in which he was to receive half of everything Frank ever made in the entertainment business. The story goes that mobster Sam Giancana made Dorsey the original "offer you can't refuse" and the contract evaporated.

World War II was going on then, and, depending on which story you believe, either Frank Sinatra was classified as 4F and rejected because of a perforated eardrum, or somebody paid his way out. In either case, while men in uniform hated him back then for not serving, girls in bobby sox loved Frank "Swoonatra," drawing huge, frenzied crowds wherever he played. Maybe as a penance, he appeared in the 1951 sappy-patriotic movie *Anchors Away*.

I saw *From Here to Eternity*, which came out in 1953, known for that infamous scene with Burt Lancaster and Deborah Kerr grinding in the surf. Frank got an Oscar for Best Supporting Actor for that movie, which he really needed because his career was in the toilet. Anyway, he got back on top, and I saw him in *The Manchurian Candidate,* which was very good, and *Von Ryan's Express,* which wasn't. There's been a hugely popular radio show here in Philly for about 60 years during which deejay Sid Marks plays only Frank's music.

At the 1967 Sinatra concert at Convention Hall, before the Spectrum opened, I bought my first wife, Myra, an album that she played over and over because it featured "Summer Wind," the song that Frank delivered to close the show.

Sinatra led a long and colorful life, and I thought I'd mention some of the highlights of his early years.

So here I am all those years later with my fancy boots up on the even fancier slab of marble desk, it's 1974 and "Frankie Boy" is coming to perform in *my* building.

The contracts for what he got paid and so forth were not my business. That was the concert promoter's job. How the building made money was my concern. That and keeping Mr. S. happy. That was no easy feat. Frank's man, Jilly Rizzo (no relation to our mayor) dictated what we had to provide.

The list was very detailed: Twelve wine glasses, six rocks glasses, four porcelain bowls, fine silverware, a double-burner hot plate, a tea kettle with spring water, a half dozen each of linen napkins and hand towels, boxes of Kleenex tissues, Ivory soap, a carton of Camels and a variety of sodas, three-quarters of which had to be diet.

You think that's a lot—and specific enough? Guess again.

We also had to provide an upright piano that had been tuned that day. Premium white and red wines and one bottle each of Jack Daniels, Chivas, Beefeaters, Stoli, Courvoisier and assorted mixers along with a case of bottled spring water.

You think Frankie was perhaps also going to be hungry?

We also had to supply one fruit platter that included watermelon, one cheese tray that included brie and Dijon mustard, two sandwiches (one turkey and one egg salad), two dozen chilled jumbo shrimp, bowls of pretzels and potato chips, a platter of Nova Scotia lox, three cans of Campbell's chicken and rice soup and—most importantly, we were informed—one bag of miniature Tootsie Rolls and a dozen boxes each of Luden's cough drops and assorted Lifesavers, especially cherry.

We did what we were told, and it paid off. Frank played our building often. Jilly told me after one concert that he didn't think Frank touched anything except the tea and the candies.

Wait, there's more!

Dressing room requirements included a "Star Dressing Room" and a selection of plants and flower arrangements "would be appreciated." There was a support act room, production office, male and female band rooms—one for exclusive use of artist's musical personnel—four telephones and an ear, nose and throat specialist on call.

With all these requirements, you would think that Sinatra was hard to work with. He wasn't. He was really committed to his craft, a perfectionist who insisted that every performance be the best.

He liked to say, "Music touches people's hearts. You know it doesn't go through your mental capacity. It just moves you and your audience at the same time."

He was usually surrounded by his entourage, which included primarily Jilly Rizzo and Jimmie Van Heusen, but he was still accessible to some of the local folks, including radio celebs Sid Marks and Jerry

Blavat. While he was cordial to the workers in my building, he rarely signed autographs or posed for pictures.

Before one show, just before his big, silver Caddy with New York plates swooshed down the Spectrum tunnel, a couple of his henchmen got out of their lead sedan and ordered the handful of laborers and arena personnel working right there to hustle into a nearby supply closet "until Mr. Sinatra passes by." They complied, but after a few minutes in the cramped room, the door suddenly opens and whose head pops in but Frank himself.

"Sorry, guys," he says apologetically. "C'mon out."

I remember another incident.

I had set up a few seats in a small area along the hockey dasher boards next to the tunnel from Frank's dressing room so I could entertain some VIPs. The stage was set up in the round in the middle of the arena. Frank's not yet on stage, and who sits down next to me and my guests but Jilly and comedian Jack Benny.

My guests and I already are impressed, and listen as Jilly tells how he had snuck Benny on Frank's private plane before they left LA and dressed him in a stewardess outfit, blonde wig and all, and sent him out to take Frank's drink order.

Sinatra has no idea who—or what—it is and whispers to Jilly, "Who's the fuckin' ugly broad?" At which point Benny doffs his wig and says, "Who'd you expect, fucking Jackie Kennedy?" Jilly says Frank doubled over in hysterics, which is what we all did as Jilly delivered the punch line.

Suddenly, the arena went dark, the orchestra hit the opening bars of "My Way" and nearly 20,000 people rose as if it was the national anthem, which, of course, it is in South Philly. Blinding spotlights picked up the Man Himself as he sprinted from the shadows, past us and up the few steps to the stage, triggering an ovation worthy of registering on the Richter Scale.

■ ■ ■

So, with all this, you wouldn't think I would allow a screw-up so major that it ended with a revolver in somebody's face. Here's the story.

I had a guy working for me who shall remain anonymous—a straight-laced accountant with a college degree, which is more than I had. Smart kid. Turns out, though, too smart for his own good. So Frank's coming in to do these two shows in about a month and his LA lawyer, Mickey Rudin, calls me himself, which is a big deal, and politely "requests" that I sell 1,000 good seats to the local Teamsters union at face value of $15 each. This is 1974 and top tickets are only

$15. He says the union is going to resell them at $30 and pocket $15K for their "charitable fund." I say "sure, Mickey," because what else can I say?

I clear it with owner Ed Snider, who's savvy enough not to question the "request," but advises me that if I ever tell anyone he knew about it, "I'll call you a liar!" Uh, thanks for the backup, Boss.

I call in my hard-eyed accountant to personally handle this request because I'm leaving in the morning for a few days in the Acapulco sun with a young sweetie that I've been chasing.

I tell him very clearly: "A guy from the Teamsters is coming by tomorrow with a check for $15,000 for one thousand good $15 seats for the first Sinatra show. A thousand good seats—not the first five rows, but good seats."

Don't worry, he says. He'll take care of it personally.

Next afternoon, an hour after my new girlfriend and I check in at the exclusive Las Brisas resort in Acapulco, we're seated at the bar in the pool and, incredulously, I hear my name paged.

"Uh-oh, this can't be good," I say.

I pick up the house phone that the bartender slides over and the hotel operator puts it through. It's my secretary, Linda, and she's in tears.

I ask what's wrong and she sobs, "There's a guy sitting in my office—with a gun! Says his name is Frankie Flowers and he's not leaving until he gets the tickets he's supposed to get."

I tell Linda to get my brilliant accountant on the phone, and I nicely ask him, "WHAT THE FUCK IS GOING ON?!"

"The tickets," he tells me, "the thousand tickets."

"You didn't do what I told you, did you?"

"I got him some other tickets, figured they didn't need such good ones."

"Put the guy on the phone," I respond, trying not to explode.

"Mr. Flowers, apparently a mix-up has occurred with your tickets while I'm out of town."

"Mix-up?" he says, "The tickets are shit."

I ask him to come back tomorrow and we'll have the right tickets ready.

"Lookit, my friend," he says, "I ain't fuckin' leavin' 'til I get the tickets we were promised. I'll just wait in your office while *you* get it right," he said, adding ominously, "and Mickey Rudin's pissed, too!"

Two things here are very bad. First, when a mobster calls you "my friend," you're in big trouble. Second, if Mickey Rudin's pissed, that's even bigger trouble.

What I didn't know at the time was that Mr. Flowers & Company already had put the arm on Electric Factory Concerts promoter Larry Magid, but got nowhere. Magid many years later related the story to the *Philadelphia Inquirer*:

"Frankie Flowers, a big-time bookmaker and florist who I casually knew called and asked for tickets for 'friends of Frank,'" Magid begins. "I said I was willing to sell him four. I think the top price was $12.50. Maybe $15. Then that Saturday, he came to my office with this other beefy guy who said he was with the Teamsters. 'Four tickets won't do, we want to buy 2,500,' Frankie told me in a soft 'good cop' voice. I told him we couldn't do this, that it would look bad to the public. And over the years we'd learned that if you say 'no' to mobsters when they try to shake you down, they usually back off.

"Not this day. Suddenly, the other guy threw himself across my desk, grabbed me by the throat, and started squeezing, choking, yelling he's going to kill me if they don't get the tickets," Magid remembered with a bitter laugh. "So now I'm starting to figure out what 'friends of Frank' really means. Still, I told them that it wasn't in my control to sell them that many tickets, as the distribution was under the Spectrum's control, which is why they then went and paid a 'social call' to the Spectrum people and put the scare on them," Magid concluded.

My financial guy, who's a whiz with figures, but, shall we say, lacked certain skills when it came to people, swears to take care of it pronto and hustles off to the box office to make the exchange.

It takes me an hour to put through two phone calls from the pool. One, to get the next plane back to Philly to put a lid on this mess. The other, to apologize to Mickey Rudin, remembering that Sinatra once said, "Don't get even. Get mad. Then get even."

Rudin's secretary puts me through, and Mickey comes on with guns blazing. "Guess what, you dick, Frank isn't playing your fucking building. He's pissed and we're going to Convention Hall in Atlantic City instead."

Oh, shit! I'm looking at two cancelled shows! I could lose my job. Or worse, wind up in a Jersey landfill. "Mickey, please accept my apologies," I stammer. "I already straightened it out and I'm gonna fire that idiot who screwed things up. Please tell Frank how sorry we are."

"Tell him yourself, he's sitting right here."

Suddenly, The Man is on the line.

'Hey, Kid," he says, "What's up?"

"Mr., uh, Sinatra," I gulp. "I can't tell you how sorry . . ."

"Don't worry about it, Kid," he interrupts, laughing. "We're just fuckin' with ya. You can buy me some 'Jack' when I'm in Philly."

He hangs up and I'm still blabbering mea culpas into a dead phone.

All of a sudden, I hear a tiny voice and remember I'm sitting on a concrete stool in a pool in my Jantzen's, overlooking gorgeous Acapulco Bay.

It's my blonde in the bikini decorating the next stool.

"Louie," she says, sounding like a ditzy Judy Holliday in *Born Yesterday*, "What's happening?"

I blow a deep sigh, order double shots of tequilas with limes and shoot her my best Humphrey Bogart:

"Doll, you don't wanna know!

"We gotta get to the airport. But first, let's hit the room and, uh, unwind."

11

In this Corner, Smokin' Joe

Boxing Is a Knock-Out

The first fight I ever saw, I was in.

Joey McDuff and I were ten or eleven and buddies, but a bunch of older boys hanging out on Joey's steps on Flora Street, including his older *schicker* brother, Petey, who kept a flask in his back pocket, goaded us into duking it out. We didn't want to fight, but they kept shoving us into each other. Scared, we went at it half-heartedly until I caught Joey on the chin by accident—and it was on.

We circled and traded punches for a minute or two, which seemed like forever, until Joey's parents came out and broke it up. One of the punks yelled, "G'wan home, you little Jew!"

Living in a Catholic neighborhood filled with blue-collar Irish, Polish and German families, I was used to being called "Jew," usually preceded with words such as "dirty," "stinkin'" or "fuckin.'"

Joey and I never spoke after that and his family stopped coming into our candy store. It was their loss, because the next closest corner store was more than two blocks away. Dumb *goyim*!

Boxing was big when I was a kid. NBC's Gillette Cavalcade of Sports fights on Friday nights was a staple of early television, featuring ranked fighters at Madison Square Garden for 14 years beginning in 1946.

My dad and I would go around the corner to Paul and Magda Chestnut's hole-in-the-wall grocery store on Stiles Street and sit in their tiny living room to watch the Friday night fights. They had one of the first home TVs in the whole area, a nine-inch Zenith—a miracle in a box.

A quart of hand-dipped Bryers bing cherry vanilla ice cream for Mr. Chestnut was the price of admission.

The Chestnuts and Al and Pearl Salkin, who had a shoe repair shop a few doors from our store, were the only other Jewish families in the neighborhood, although the Rothsteins had a corner butcher shop across 30th Street for a while. I attended Sunday school and was Bar Mitzvah'd at Keneseth Israel Reformed Synagogue at Broad Street and Columbia Avenue. The building later was sold to Temple University and Columbia Avenue has been renamed for Cecil B. Moore, the late Black activist and flamboyant Philadelphia lawyer. (I got to know "Cecil B" pretty well in my reporting days, a great guy to hang out with.) We weren't very religious, didn't keep a kosher house and since my parents were born in Philadelphia, we didn't speak Yiddish. We enjoyed ham sandwiches, but the first time I tasted bacon was in my freshman year at TU when I heard someone order a BLT. I tried one—and have been hooked ever since.

At the time, heavyweight champ Joe Louis, the Brown Bomber, was a towering figure in American sports. He was a Free World hero for knocking out Hitler's favorite boxer Max Schmeling in 1938, avenging an earlier loss to the one-time Nazi puppet, in bouts that captured global interest.

We were excited when Camden's Jersey Joe Walcott, whose real name was Arnold Cream, got a chance to fight Joe Louis on December 5, 1947. Walcott was a good fighter with 44 wins, 11 losses, 2 draws—and a deep 10--1 underdog for this event. Louis was 57–1 and had won 32 consecutive bouts, mostly by knockout.

I was 12 years old and dying to see the fight, but my dad had to tend to the store, the Chestnuts weren't home and the closest place with a TV set was at Schellhardt's corner saloon across the street.

We knew Max and Annie Schellhardt and their passel of kids, but my parents weren't drinkers and I had never been in the bar. Around 10:00 the night of the fight, I got up courage, crossed busy Girard Avenue, pushed open the taproom door and peeked in. The fight already was on and the place was packed and noisy. White men lined the bar, smoking, yelling and cursing. The place reeked of spilled beer and body odor. I took a few steps inside.

Nobody noticed me at first. Then, a big guy on a bar stool slid off, grabbed me and lifted me onto his lap. I was little and skinny and probably looked about eight.

"Here, kid," he said. "Up here so you can see."

I watched as Jersey Joe outboxed the champ, sending the place into bedlam by knocking Louis onto the canvas twice, on his way to an apparent huge upset. The fight went the full 15 rounds and Walcott was clearly the better fighter. But in one of the classic rip-offs in boxing history, the two judges voted for Louis and only referee Ruby Goldstein scored it right, with Walcott ahead. The bar erupted!

Convinced that he had lost and disgusted with his performance, Louis had tried to leave the ring before the decision but was held back by his corner. The champ was stunned as was most everyone else at Madison Square Garden.

Afterwards, Louis handled himself with uncommon class. "I don't know what the judges were watching because I got beat," he told a reporter. "He deserves the win."

Six months later, they fought again, this time in Yankee Stadium, and Louis kayoed Jersey Joe in the 11th round.

My dad had taken me to see boxing at the old Arena when I was nine or ten, but the cigar and cigarette smoke was so bad that I could hardly see the ring from the cheap seats.

Later on, working the Arena box office for boxing matches was rough if somebody—sometimes a lot of somebodies—wanted their money back, particularly if fights didn't turn out to their liking. Fighters who weren't the headliners or high up on the card got paid in tickets, and more times than not, they tried to cash in the ones they couldn't sell. The one rule that I was given was *never* to refund any money to any one at any time.

A lot of famous boxers fought at the Arena including Joey Giardello, Gil Turner and my favorite, Jack O'Halloran, who went on to be in the movies, including *Superman*. Others included Nate Gold, Georgie Benton and a group they called the Philly Fighters: Gypsy Joe Harris (who was blind in one eye), Bennie Briscoe (who wore a Jewish star on his trunks but wasn't), Kitten Hayward, Willie the Worm Monroe and Smokin' Joe Frazier, who became the heavyweight champion of the world and was the first sports headliner at my building years later.

By the time the Spectrum opened, the bigger fights were being held at Convention Hall and the smaller ones split between the Arena and the Blue Horizon, the cramped, legendary boxing hall on Broad Street near Temple.

The first fight card we put on at the Spectrum was on October 17, 1967, staged by veteran Philly promoter Herman Taylor. Joe Frazier, up from South Carolina, a gold medal winner in the 1964 Olympics and trying to quit his job in a Philly slaughterhouse, battered Tony Doyle. A crowd of about 8,000 brought in $51,000, and Tony from Utah made it into the second round before one of Joe's devastating left hooks made "Doyle come apart like a shattered mirror," as one sportswriter wrote.

The next year featured Emile Griffith, who later came out as gay, winning in 12 rounds over Gypsy Joe Harris. Griffith went on to beat Benny "Kid" Parrot to death in the ring for calling him "a queer." Gypsy Joe, blind in one eye, went on to be a garbage man after the State Athletic Commission ruled he was too visually impaired to continue fighting.

Two months later, one of the fabulous Philadelphia middle-weights, Kitten Hayward, went the distance to steal a win from Griffith. We did very well with the concessions, the site fee and a gate of over $120,000 for the first fight. The promoters also did well. We finished out the year with Frazier getting off the canvas twice to earn a 15-round decision and a minor title over rugged Oscar Bonavena, whose public life was later somewhat curtailed at age 34 by being shot to death outside a brothel in Nevada.

The Spectrum had few boxing cards until J. Russell Peltz began his tenure as our boxing chief at the tail end of 1972. Peltz was fascinated by boxing. When he was about 12, he went to a boxing match "instead of studying for his bar mitzvah," his mother said. He graduated as a journalism major from Temple University and worked the sports desk for the *Evening Bulletin*.

He started his promoting career with a card at the Blue Horizon on September 30, 1969. "Bad" Bennie Briscoe, who might have been as good as Philly's Bernard Hopkins, scored a first-round knockout in front of a standing-room-only crowd of 1,600. Russell staged several local shows at the Arena and the Blue Horizon, using his skills as a matchmaker to draw decent numbers.

I approached him in December 1972 and said I was working on putting up $1 million a year for 50 "Monday Night Fights," offering generous $20,000 purses per show to bring in good boxers. To say Russell was excited is putting it mildly. I thought he'd have a stroke.

I promised I'd get back to him before the end of the month, cautioning that I had to get the deal approved, which wasn't going to be a snap. Mondays were usually dark at the Spectrum and I needed to find something to fill the seats.

It took me until after 10:00 p.m. on New Year's Eve to finalize it over the phone with Ed Snider. I convinced the boss that the million dollars was a PR device and that if we couldn't at least break even on ticket sales, plus sponsorships, parking and concessions revenue, I'd pull the plug after a month.

"You really believe in this, huh?"

"I do."

"Enough to make up any losses out of your pay?"

"Absolutely," I lied.

"It'd better work," he said, knowing that he'd never deduct a dime.

Driving home, I tried Peltz from my car, but it was the early days of car phones and I had to wait almost 20 minutes to get a signal tone.

He answered like a man going to the guillotine.

"Russell, I told you I'd get back to you."

"I thought it was dead already," he said.

"Only if you don't want to be the Spectrum's first Director of Boxing."

There's this panic, and he's yelling to his wife and they're both whooping it up.

Now, all I had to do was make it work.

We had a Spectrum Fights logo designed. And keychains with little boxing gloves. And hot ring card girls in tight tees making appearances around town. And we promoted the hell out of it on Flyers broadcasts and after the PRISM channel launched in 1976. Spectrum promotions director Jay Seidman plastered the town with fight posters at area gyms, ticket broker offices, stores and bars. We gave comp tickets to stars on the Philly teams to dress up ringside alongside area celebs, politicians and fine-looking ladies that we came across.

Jay was a one-man gang, lining up crowd-pleasing events at the matches, including boxing kangaroos, Indian fakirs lying on beds of nails and a guy named Bennie the Bomb, who blew himself up!

Peltz was a purist and the wild antics drove him nuts, but we insisted on putting on a show. He was prolific at arranging competitive matches, but we lost money on 15 of his first 18 shows. The program was in jeopardy, as was Russell's job, until he insisted Philly fighters start fighting Philly fighters. After that, things went through the roof.

We had a total of 15 fight dates in our first six years before Peltz. He put on 16 in 1973 and 11 each in 1974 and 1975. It was a Golden Age with world-class fighters like Briscoe and Marvin Hagler filling the house, drawing 15,000 in August of 1978. There was also Tyrone Everett v. Briscoe in 1975, which brought in 60 grand, and Mike "The Jewish Bomber" Rossman, who later won the light-heavyweight title, bringing in $118,000.

The matches were run first class, with clean dressing rooms instead of the rat-holes that fighters and managers were used to. Parking was easy and concession stands had decent food at decent prices.

Most important, we made honest pay-outs at the end of the night. Our finance guys would sit down in a conference room after the bouts and go over the numbers with no phony bullshit charges. The purses were guaranteed, which was a lot stricter than paying somebody who was getting his head beat in by giving him tickets to sell or a percentage of the gate, which could be anything a promoter wanted it to be.

There would be the guarantee, less taxes, State Boxing Commission fees, and their manager's cut, all of which had to be agreed to in advance. Then we'd write a check right there and if the fighters wanted, we'd cash it for them. Sometimes we'd even help them slip out of the building past angry ex-wives, girlfriends, hangers-on, debt collectors and potential muggers—all waiting to grab a piece of a hard-earned purse.

Not that the events themselves were easy to put on. They were nerve-wracking and scary. Peltz was a worrywart who would check every detail again and again and pace back and forth at ringside. More than once, a fighter either failed to show up or was grabbed by the cops for an outstanding warrant as he headed for the ring.

The box office was often a nightmare with lots of last-minute walk-ups buying tickets and a goodly portion of the patrons already half in the bag. We had to handle bouts that weren't in the ring, especially among boxers' fans and families, which happened more than you'd think. And there was always the possibility of a full-fledged donnybrook matching Black against white or Eastwick brawling with Kensington.

A scheduled fighter from South Philly against somebody from North Philly drew blood-thirsty fans. Even better was when you had two fighters from the same neighborhood, like on July 15, 1974, when Bobby "Boogaloo" Watts went against Eugene "Cyclone" Hart, who had 19 straight knockouts, for the unofficial North Philly crown. Boogaloo won by a kayo in the very first round. It was good for the fighters, the city and our cash registers.

Closed-circuit TV for big fights meant big money for the Spectrum, produced locally by a classy Joe Hand, Sr. The biggest of them involved, among others, famed heavyweights Muhammed Ali, Joe Frazier, George Foreman and Ken Norton.

Super Fight II, the non-title match on January 28, 1974 between Ali and Frazier at Madison Square Garden, was the second of three epic bouts. However, we already had the city's annual indoor track meet championships booked for that night. The Philadelphia Recreation Department scheduled the meet a year ahead of time as it was its most important event.

In fact, when the Spectrum was being designed, Recreation Commissioner Bob Crawford, whose department provided support of the arena with landscaping, fencing and other exterior improvements, requested that we install movable floor stands that could be rolled back to create a seven-lap, indoor mile oval.

The Ali-Frazier bout, announced several weeks before the track meet, was too big to turn away, but we couldn't reschedule the city's marquee event, which drew contestants and media from across the nation.

I told Ed Snider, "We'll do both!"

Ed was skeptical. "How are you going to pull that off?"

The track meet normally would draw maybe eight or nine thousand fans, but the building could hold nearly 20 thousand, which we'd fill for a big TV fight.

"We'll continue to sell track tickets at six and ten bucks," I said, "for early afternoon admission when the meet starts—and twice that to come in after seven o'clock toward the end of the Rec Department's event. The fight telecast wouldn't begin until after eight, with the main event around ten o'clock."

The fight tickets quickly sold out the rest of the house. A larger than usual crowd cheered on the track finals and in short time, a packed house awaited the fights. Outside, more than a thousand fight fans milled about, looking to buy tickets, but the ticket windows were shut, and the doors closed and guarded. That didn't stop several hundred fans from crashing through the glass doors to the lower-level executive offices.

I was right there as the mob broke through but didn't know where to go. I hustled our young switchboard operator out of their path and yelled, "THAT WAY!!"—pointing to the service corridor under the stands, which led to the event floor.

Thankfully, they stampeded in that direction with neither hesitation nor incident. I radioed ahead to security to let them through since there was plenty of room to sit on the track. I didn't care that they got in free. Nobody got hurt, nobody got busted—and they were only looking to buy tickets in the first place. The night went off without another hitch, with the intruders shoulder to shoulder sitting on the floor with scores of track athletes enjoying the telecast.

Ali won by unanimous decision, though criticized for clutching and grabbing the entire night. The Spectrum had a massive payday and the Recreation Department wound up with its biggest check ever.

"How'd it go?" Ed asked me the next day.

"No problem," I said.

"Who won?"

"We did!"

Then a couple of things happened that neither Russell Peltz nor I nor a whole ring full of champions could have stopped.

First, TV's Monday Night Football debuted with Howard Cosell, "Dandy" Don Meredith and Frank Gifford (who everybody from Philadelphia knows was knocked out cold by Concrete Charlie Bednarik) and delivered a wicked body blow to our program. Then, the casinos in Atlantic City finished us off by booking mega bouts on a regular basis.

The building had one last hurrah in 1995 when Iron Mike Tyson, who was banned in New Jersey, started his post-prison comeback by demolishing Buster Mathis in our ring.

And Bernard "the Executioner" Hopkins, maybe Philly's best in the modern era, defended his title at the Spectrum in 2003 with a TKO of Morrade Hakkar in the eighth round. There were a couple of cards in 2005 and 2006, but big-time boxing in Philly was finished.

Now in his 70s, Peltz celebrated 50 years in boxing in 2019 and before the pandemic continued to earn a good buck promoting competitive matches in and around Philadelphia, in casinos and at the 2300 Arena in South Philly, which holds about 1,300 fans and gets its name from its address on South Swanson Street. Locals might know the building from its former names: Viking Hall, Alhambra Arena, the Arena and Asylum Arena.

Peltz is still a purist who insists on presenting bouts solely among evenly matched fighters, which is why most of his shows are standing room only and why he's lasted half a century in a sleazy business. He has stuck religiously to his standards, never wavering even a little.

Which is more than many of us can say.

12

God Bless Kate

Lady Luck Fills the Cups

In the spring of 1938, Hitler was plundering Europe and America was in the Depression. We were being drawn into a fearsome global war and our nation was full of worry.

It was before TV, when American families would gather around their radios. Moms and Dads listened to the foreboding evening news and then tuned to all our favorite shows. Radio was the nation's mass entertainment, and its biggest star of them all was Kate Smith, known as "the Songbird of the South."

She was a fiercely proud American, saddened that people were worried about their futures, and she wanted to make things better. So Kate asked the great Irving Berlin, who wrote "White Christmas" and dozens of other classics, if he could pen a patriotic song for her that might lift the country's spirit. Berlin remembered a song he had written 21 years earlier during World War I, but never got around to publishing. It was called "God Bless America."

He graciously gave it to her, asking only that any profits derived from it go to one of his favorite charities, the Boy Scouts of America. (For generations, the Boy Scouts and later, Girl Scouts, have been receiving millions of dollars in royalties—and still do.)

Kate brought the song to her CBS Radio studio in New York to work on it with her orchestra, and on November 10, 1938, she sang it to a live studio audience and to millions of listeners around the world for the first time. There's actually footage available on YouTube of the song's debut on the *Kate Smith Hour* radio show.

Thirty-one years later, in 1969, the mood across the land again was anything but cheerful. America was gripped in another sort of malaise as civil unrest over the Vietnam War and bitter racial issues were tearing at the collective fabric of our lives. The draft lottery was reinstated for the first time since World War II, and President Nixon sent 50,000 additional troops into the raging, bloody jungle conflict. The Tet Offensive was pushing the Americans backwards for nearly a year with devastating results and no end in sight. Fifty-eight thousand of our brave young soldiers didn't make it home alive. Many more returned a mess physically and mentally.

Racial tensions were at fever pitch. The Supreme Court ordered Mississippi to desegregate its schools. Students clashed violently on campus with police and the military, demanding an end to the war. The nation still was reeling from the shock of the assassinations of President John F. Kennedy, Martin Luther King, Jr. and Bobby Kennedy.

On the job at the Spectrum, I was disheartened as fans at Flyers and 76ers games were apathetic or rude when the national anthem was played, sitting, chatting, eating, not removing hats, some even enjoying a smoke of exotic origins.

I wondered how they'd feel if the "Star Spangled Banner" was taken away from them and thought about playing something else to shake things up. I wasn't sure what song to use as a replacement, but knew I had the right one when I found Kate's 1938 rendition on a vinyl record in a dusty bin at a used record store on South Street.

The next day, I asked the electrician in the Spectrum sound booth to play it for me a few times. He had to first convert the old LP vinyl record to reel-to-reel tape to fit our new system, played it inside his booth and eagerly agreed to a few hours of overtime to stay past 5:00 p.m. Then, the building would be empty and dark so I could hear the song over the arena's big public address speakers.

Without revealing my intent, I had him play it several times as I moved from the lower level to the second deck and to the far reaches in the corners to hear how it carried throughout the building. I closed my eyes and tried to picture the building packed with 15,000 fans and the skaters at attention along the blue lines.

I got goosebumps each time Kate hit that powerful, impossibly high "home, sweet home" ending. Hearing it echo through the vast, deserted auditorium got my heart pounding, and I found myself sweating with excitement. This was no small thing to contemplate, but what could be more patriotic? If this didn't do the trick—and maybe get the underdog Flyers jacked up to win a game—what would?

But I needed to know more. I did some research at the big library on the Benjamin Franklin Parkway and learned that Irving Berlin grew up hearing his mother, Katherine, exclaim "God bless America" many times. He said she uttered it with such great emotion that it seemed "like an exaltation" in their tiny New York City apartment, where they had settled after the family had fled Russia's persecution of Jews in 1893.

His daughter, Mary Ellin Barrett, said her dad meant every word in the song. "It *was* the land he truly loved. It was his home sweet home," she said.

Berlin, born Israel Beilin, was five years old when a Jew-hunting Soviet mob burned his house to the ground and the family began a trek that eventually led to America. Twenty-five years later, the same year he became a naturalized U.S. citizen, he wrote the song. He was a soldier stationed at Camp Upton in New York State and wrote it as the finale for a camp revue. He decided not to use it and forgot about it until dusting it off for Ms. Smith.

I asked the sound electrician to hold it for "possible use" and to see whether the track, scratchy in spots, could be cleaned up. He'd said he'd try his best and asked me what I had in mind.

"I'm not sure," I said, which was no lie, because I didn't know whether I would actually do it. "I'll let you know, maybe in a few days."

The Flyers were in their second year of existence and woefully inexperienced. Wins were hard to come by, especially against the more talented six original teams from Montreal, Toronto, New York, Boston, Chicago and Detroit. I looked at the schedule and saw that the powerful Toronto Maple Leafs were coming in the following week. That was what we called a "money game": A glamor team, larger crowd, plenty of VIPs, and it would be broadcast regionally and across Canada.

That day, January 11, 1969, at about 4:00 p.m., I left my office in the lower level of the Spectrum without mentioning anything to anyone and strolled up the hall and down the players' tunnel to the ice. I looked up and around as cleaners and tradesmen readied the building and ice surface and stocked the concession stands. I took one look at all the TV cameras, local and from Canada, that were already in position, the radio booth being set up, and the larger-than-usual press contingent already typing away—and decided to pull the trigger.

Back in my office, I called the sound booth and asked to have the tape queued up by 6:45 p.m. The doors would be opened by 6:00 p.m. and game time was 7:05. A few minutes before 7:00, using the overhead in-house phone in the Super Box, I called down to PA announcer Kevin Johnson (Lou Nolan didn't become announcer until 1972) and gave him a heads up.

"You're kidding," he said.

Then I alerted the sound booth.

"Are you for real?" the electrician asked.

I assured them both that I was dead serious, and within a few minutes, with players from both sides lined up along their blue lines, I heard Kevin's words booming over the huge speakers:

"LADIES AND GENTLEMEN, WOULD YOU PLEASE RISE AND JOIN IN SINGING KATE SMITH'S RECORDING OF GOD BLESS AMERICA."

My heart was beating like crazy and my brow covered in perspiration. I had no idea how this was going to turn out, but it was too late to do anything but stand there—and take whatever came.

There was an eerie hush, followed by a "what the . . . ?" murmur that swept the stands. I heard a few derisive shouts. But by the time Kate's amazing voice hit that off-the-charts last note, the crowd was fully abuzz.

Ed Snider, the Flyers', uh, rather intense owner, was shocked. He whipped around, glared at me, bolted from his seat and stormed half the length of the 60-seat Super Box to where I stood. His face afire, he informed me in colorful terms what he thought of my latest brainstorm.

"I told you I was thinking about it," I replied, holding my ground.

"But I didn't think you were crazy enough to actually do it!" he shouted. "This time you've gone too goddamned far!"

The Flyers shot out of the gate hustling, fighting and scoring, with the crowd roaring on most every shift. At the end of the first period, fans streamed up the aisle past the owner's seat smiling at "Mister Snider" and telling him how great the team looked. One even suggested the song may have brought good luck. By the end of a crackling good game in which the Flyers skated hard, hit often and won 6–3, fans passing Ed's box among the announced crowd of 10,059 told the boss how much they loved the song, shook his hand and congratulated him on playing it.

One woman said, "Mr. Snider, this great song should be our national anthem."

I clocked the action deadpan from my perch about 50 feet away.

Ed finally got up, came over sporting a disbelieving smile and shook his head.

"I don't know how you pulled this off, you crazy sonuvabitch," he said, hugging me. "But keep it up."

Next day a *Philadelphia Inquirer* writer snickered that since the Flyers, losers of eight of its previous nine games, had won one in a row with Kate Smith, "they might want to keep her in the lineup!"

Thus, was born the magical, improbable love affair between Kate Smith and "her boys," a collection of toothless, colorful Broad Street Bullies from Canada wearing the orange and black. The songbird quickly became a cherished member of the Flyers family and a Philly icon, and saw her career, heretofore in decline, resurrected.

I played "God Bless America" only 21 times over the first three seasons—solely for key games—and it worked like a charm. Of the 21 times I directed it be used, the Flyers won 19 of those games, tied one and lost only once, light years away from their dismal losing records in those days. (By the end of the 2018–19 season, her record stood at a sparkling 101–31–5.)

Of course, my next move was to try to get Kate Smith to sing it live in the Spectrum. It wasn't easy. It would be four long years from the first time it was played before we could get her to perform on the ice before an out-of-their-minds adoring crowd at a Flyers game at the Spectrum.

Her snooty agent Raymond Katz flatly dismissed our many calls to his office.

"Miss Smith sings for presidents and kings, the Pope," he sniffed, "not for a hockey game."

Jay Seidman, who helped pump up the Monday Night Fights program, dogged Katz with no luck, until fate intervened. Turned out that Kate had an elderly uncle living in, of all places, West Philly, who, at the end of the 1972–73 season, sent her news clippings of her Flyers' good luck streak. Kate showed them to her agent and asked whether he thought the Flyers would let her come perform it in person. He sheepishly told her we had been extending invitations and she immediately told him to make the arrangements.

It was a few days after Labor Day 1973, with all of us back at our desks, when Jay ran into my office with the big news. We got Katz back on the phone.

"Against my better judgment, Miss Smith has deigned to appear," he said condescendingly from his lofty Manhattan offices.

"She gets $25,000 an appearance," he informed us, "which you can't possibly afford [this was about $175,000 in today's dollars], but make an offer that doesn't insult me."

We said we could pay $5000.

"That's an insult," he huffed.

We held firm.

He took it to Miss Smith, whose legendary career had been winding down, and she eagerly agreed. It was a feel-good story, something new and exciting for the great Miss Smith. I think she would have come for train fare and a couple of Pat's cheesesteaks.

Next day, I mosey into Ed Snider's office and after some other business, bring up Kate's amazing winning skein.

"You know," he says, "We should try to get her here in person."

Ya think?

"As a matter of fact," I reply, "We do have her coming."

"That's fantas—" he starts, but interrupts himself. "How much?"

"Ten thousand dollars," I tell him.

"Holy shit," he shakes his head. "We can't afford that."

I wait as he thinks hard. He knows this is too big to pass up.

"Ok," he says, "We've got to do it. I'll find the money somehow."

"Good," I say, "because it's really only $5,000."

"You sonovabitch!" he blurts.

"Hey, I just saved you $5,000—and you're cursing me out?"

We break up laughing.

That's the kind of relationship Ed and I had. We loved the joust of give and take. Sometimes he nailed me. Other times I got him. More importantly, we got each other.

I figured the best game for her live appearance would be our home opener on October 11, 1973, against those same Toronto Maple Leafs. She was going to be on the East Coast and available. Jay made the deal with Katz, but we told no one other than Ed.

Kate arrives with a small green suitcase and her organist by train from New York about 5:00 p.m. We send limo driver John Foreman to 30th Street Station to get her, but to keep it quiet. Big John, who is about 6'5" and nearly 300 pounds, slips them in through the back door of my office without fanfare, and I can see the excitement in Kate's eyes. It is unreal to actually have this great woman and international legend in my office. We hug warmly, chat for a bit and then Jay shows her to a dressing room down the hall—but in minutes, Kate is back with bad news.

"I can't go on," she says. "My gown is totally creased."

No problem, I explain. We'll iron it.

We scour the building, but turns it out we don't have an iron anywhere.

I buzz my secretary, Maria Milano, a wonderful South Philly girl. She tells me her aunt Kay has an iron, and better yet, she lives only a few blocks from the Spectrum. Maria calls Aunt Kay and tells her the deal, but asks her not to say anything. With the clock ticking, Maria gives Big John the dress and off he goes to Aunt Kay's house.

Of course, by the time the gown is ironed, hung on a velvet hanger, zipped into a garment bag and handed to Big John, there's a dozen neighbors waiting on Aunt Kay's pavement to see Kate Smith's dress. The sight of Big John and a big black limo on the narrow South Philly street kind of drew attention, too. Good thing cell phones weren't around.

At exactly 7:00 p.m., a red carpet is unfurled from the Zamboni tunnel onto the Spectrum ice. An organ and bench are wheeled out. Surely, this sell-out record crowd of 17,007, filling every inch of the building, including its brand-new third level, expects Kate's good-luck recording.

But wait . . . could it be?

The throng rises expectantly. A ripple becomes a roar. The house lights dim. The stands come alive. Xenon spotlights snap on as the accompanist takes his seat. The arena is nutso.

"Ladies and gentlemen," Lou Nolan booms, "Would you please rise and join KATE SMITH . . ." The rest of his words drown in a sea of sound as the beloved lady herself appears, bathed in spotlights from every direction.

The building shakes from stomping feet and the deep, prolonged din as Kate, resplendent in her freshly ironed gown, basks in their adulation, throwing kisses. A blitzkrieg of flashes from Kodak Instamatics and other fan cameras bathe the darkened stands like a zillion fireflies.

Up in the Super Box, I stand next to Ed Snider and our wives with lumps in our throats.

Lou Nolan tells me later that it was one of the most thrilling moments of his career.

Finally, with the crowd quieter, her magnificent voice filled the air.

Maple Leaf goalie Doug Favell, a former Flyer, said that when the red carpet was rolled out, "I knew we were cooked!" And cooked they were, losing 2–0 to his mentor, Flyers goalie Bernie Parent.

By the time Kate finished, with ovations thundering from the rafters, you could barely hear her final notes. Spectrum security guards escorted her up to our box. She was crying, obviously deeply moved and a bit shaken.

"I've sung all over the world," she began, "but this—" —gesturing at the stands. "I've never had such an ovation."

I grew up in the 1940s listening to her radio show with my parents on a little General Electric radio behind the counter of our candy store. My folks idolized her, especially during the war, when she traveled extensively to raise hundreds of millions of dollars in U.S. war bonds for America's military effort.

This instant, I was beyond proud to show this global icon to her seat—next to my parents, Alexander and Frances and my wife, Myra, seated right behind a beaming Ed Snider and his wife, Myrna.

Whatta night!

Kate's appearance set the tone for the season as the Flyers recorded a gaudy 50 wins, 12 ties and only 16 losses, and skated into the NHL finals against Boston.

Leading the final series three games to two against the heavily favored Bruins, we brought Kate Smith back to the Spectrum for the key sixth game to sing. It was pretty much a must-win situation because a loss meant having to travel to Boston for a game seven, and facing the star-laden Bruins on their home ice at hostile Boston Gardens, where they would be almost unbeatable.

I remember TV celeb Mike Douglas, a Cleveland transplant, calling me and offering to sing the national anthem prior to the game. Douglas, a big star with an ego to match, hosted his national show out of Channel 3 studios in Philadelphia, but apparently hadn't been paying attention.

I told him we had "someone else" lined up for the spot, and he asked if he could come to the game to be introduced. Sorry, Mike, never saw you at a Flyers game before and no seats available.

Naturally, the crowd goes cardiac when the red carpet is rolled out, followed by the organ and a burst of spotlights.

When Kate finishes, Boston greats Bobby Orr and Phil Esposito, who had anticipated the moment, skate over and hand her bouquets of flowers. As she is escorted off the ice, Kate tells the guards how sweet it was of "our boys to give me flowers." Informed that it was the Bruins who presented them, Kate is at first shocked, then recovers and throws the flowers in a nearby trash can.

The Flyers went on to beat Boston, 1–0, to win the first of their two successive Stanley Cup Championships. They would go to the finals a few more times over the next 45 years (through 2021), but haven't recaptured the Stanley Cup.

Kate's appearance that afternoon drew an obscenity-laced tirade after the game from Bruins coach Bep Guidolin, even though several Bruins lauded Smith's elegance as a performer. He was a sore loser who didn't appreciate the theatrics.

She would make two more live appearances at the Spectrum, belting out "our" national anthem before games. When she passed away on June 17, 1986 at age 79 from diabetes, Ed Snider was one of her pallbearers. A year later, Ed had a statue installed in her honor outside the Spectrum.

Sadly, in 2019, three years following the death of Ed Snider, the statue was removed by the Flyers' owners, Comcast Spectacor, amid a controversy over lyrics some considered racial in two songs she performed as a young singer some 90 years before. At the time, corporate officials said her rendition of "God Bless America" would be banned, ending a unique fan-favorite duet with the late Miss Smith shown on the videoboard while Flyers anthemist Lauren Hart sang live.

If all good things must come to an end, I guess this was as good a magical run as any. She thrilled and inspired millions around the globe as an American hero and received the Presidential Medal of Freedom in 1982.

How do I feel about her treatment after her demise? Like legions of Americans, I'm disappointed, especially in the heavy-handed way she was dumped. Yanking the song and clumsily covering the statue before removing it in the middle of the night was harsh but, considering the later historic Black Lives Matter protests of 2020, perhaps the owners were prescient.

Many have asked me what the passionate owner Ed Snider would have done. That's hard to say, but I know he had an iron backbone and at the very least would have taken the time to handle it more respectfully, especially when you recall his words at her funeral:

"She was a wonderful person and an important part of the Flyers' history. We will always have a special place in our hearts for her. She will be deeply missed by the Flyers and our fans."

Little did he know just how much.

13

The Flyers Win the City!

We Walk Together Forever

The huge parade down Broad Street in May 1974 in front of two million crazed fans suddenly came to a halt.

Bernie Parent had to pee.

His open convertible braked near the 1500 block of South Broad, and cops rushed in like Moses to part the orange sea so the Stanley Cup MVP goalie could enter a random, lucky house to relieve himself. "The combination of excitement and beer got to me," he said, "so I jumped out of the car and started to head for one of the houses."

The monster crowd was adoring but unrestrained, and things got crazy. Fans had been pawing at their hockey gods riding in the open cars, even yanking the sleeve off Don "Big Bird" Saleski's sports jacket. Beer in hand, fans had been dodging police all along the route to shake hands with the players. A beer can hit Bobby Clarke on his beat-up leg, fans grabbed at him and at his wife, Sandy, and they fled the parade to safety.

With Bernie on the loose, six cops immediately surrounded him, with one of the officers handcuffing him to his own wrist so he couldn't be pulled away. They hustled him into the first house that the owners giddily offered up. The family was thrilled to have Bernie hit their head. Word was they even had their MVP (Most Valued Porcelain) bronzed. This was probably the most publicized Philly leak in which the urinator didn't get busted.

The wildly popular "Broad Street Bullies" had galvanized a depressed city with their toughness and charisma, lifting a beaten-down region's spirits, finally giving them something to celebrate.

"We were a blue-collar team in a blue-collar town," Parent said, "and they loved the way we played." This, from a bunch of Canadians with missing teeth who grew up playing in front of small crowds in small towns.

When the Flyers won the Stanley Cup again a year later, City Hall was better prepared, loading the team onto long, flatbed trucks where the fans couldn't reach them, even though they tried.

In the second parade, Bernie wound up standing next to Mayor Frank Rizzo at the front of one of the trucks and noticed the controversial former police commissioner scanning rooftops.

"What are you looking for?" Bernie asked.

"Snipers," said Rizzo.

Bernie gulped and moved as far away from the Mayor as he could.

That second championship was as good as it got for the brilliant, trophy-winning netminder, acknowledged as having the finest consecutive goal-tending seasons in league history.

The next few years, he was hit with devastating injuries. First, a pinched nerve in his neck in the 1975–76 season sent bolts of pain radiating through his upper body and resulted basically in a lost season. The high-risk operation on Bernie's neck was performed successfully by eminent surgeon Dr. Fred Simeone, better known today for his world-famous Simeone Foundation Automotive Museum located near the Philadelphia airport.

Then, in 1979, there was a freak injury when the angled blade of a New York Rangers errant stick managed to slice through the narrow slit of his mask and rip into his right eye. Bernie dashed off the ice in unimaginable pain and fear, ripping off his mask as blood poured down his face.

He never played again. Nor did he ever regain full vision in that eye. In fact, the shock of the blow rendered him completely blind for days.

All Bernie knew was hockey. It was his life and, at age 34, when most athletes come into their prime, he was hardly prepared for what came next. In short, he drowned himself in beer, became an alcoholic, blew his funds on unwise expenditures including a fishing yacht that would be repossessed, discovered that his agent had squandered his savings on bad investments, and lost his wife in divorce.

All of this to the sweetest, most positive and decent human being you'd ever meet.

Ed Snider supported him financially and emotionally, and eventually got him back on the ice in a meaningful way as a coach of goalies. This was something into which the fallen Flyers hero could comfortably and confidently sink his teeth. Bernie eventually figured it out, quit partying and pulled himself together. He's been sober for more than 40 years and is happily remarried to Gini Gramaglia, a beautiful, vivacious woman who owns a hair design studio for cancer patients. Bernie makes scores of public appearances every year—and of this writing remains on the Flyers payroll as an ambassador.

What's more, he still has that mischievous twinkle, smiles broadly at friends and fans on the street and (pandemics aside) gives giant, lusty bear hugs freely and often. Bernie was elected to the NHL Hall of Fame in 1984 and named one of the 100 greatest ever to play the game.

I wouldn't be exaggerating if I said I totally love this guy. He is a treasure, and Philadelphia is fortunate to have him.

■ ■ ■

Few gave the young Flyers a chance in the 1973–74 Stanley Cup Finals against the favored Boston Bruins, but their star center, Phil Esposito, sounded a warning: "Hey, that team won 50 games, so they must be doing something right." The Flyers regular season record was 50 wins, 16 losses and 12 ties.

We, too, had our doubts, going from a raw, rag-tag expansion team to deep into the playoffs in only our seventh season. After dispatching the Atlanta Flames in a four-game sweep, the Flyers had the formidable New York Rangers next.

"I just hope we don't get embarrassed," Ed Snider confided on the eve of the first game.

We needn't have worried. The Flyers eliminated the Blue Shirts in seven games. Then it was on to Boston for the finals. We lost the first game, 3–2, but stunned Bean Town in the next game with a dramatic 3–2 overtime victory when Bobby Clarke, the club's heart and soul, scored, leaped into the air, and into a photograph for the ages.

Home for the next two games, the Flyers out-hustled and out-hit the over-confident Bruins, 4–1 and 4–2. Back in Boston for game five, Boston poured it on, winning 5–1, setting up the dramatic sixth game at the Spectrum.

By now, Philly and the hockey world were caught up in the exploits of this badass gang on skates. We rolled out the red carpet and organ for Kate Smith's second of four live Spectrum appearances—

and the old gal, with some help from an invincible Parent, came through. Rick MacLeish scored the only goal of the game and the Flyers won 1–0, setting off a raucous, frenzied celebration as hundreds of spectators, including "Fan No. 1" Ed Snider, raced down the steps, scrambled over the glass and onto the rink to mob the players.

"We never really got the chance to skate around the ice in a victory lap with the Stanley Cup," said Parent. The locker room was bedlam with press, players' families, Mayor Rizzo, Kate Smith and even some ballsy fans packed wall to wall. Snider, Clarke, Parent, Andre "Moose" Dupont and others took turns pouring beer into the top of the Stanley Cup and savoring the drink of drinks.

I don't think there was much champagne sprayed—mostly beer, cases of it. The sartorially splendid Snider was soaked through with sweat and beer and giddily exhausted.

Winning the Stanley Cup the following year against the Buffalo Sabres showed the world that the Flyers were for real, bully-ball notwithstanding. Sure, they could fight, but they also could skate like hell. Their grind and grit captivated an underdog town, created a lusty tribal following across North America and, along the way, converted haters in Canada. They even managed to piss off Russia when they manhandled the vaunted Red Army team at the Spectrum in a 1976 showdown televised around the globe.

Every game brought packed houses, home and away. Most every team brought their "A" game when the Flyers skated into their town but showed up timid when visiting the Spectrum. Philly writers said teams coming into the Spectrum suddenly got the "Flyers Flu." One Canadian newspaper, anticipating the Flyers' arrival, posted a headline, "Get the women and children off the street, the Flyers are coming!"

We loved it. The press loved it. And our fans couldn't get enough.

Some visiting players decided to sit it out, while others who played were intimidated by Philly's knuckle sandwich style and hellacious hits from Gary Dornhoefer and Ed Van Impe as well as the thunderous fists of Dave "The Hammer" Schultz, Bob "Hound" Kelly, Don "Big Bird" Saleski and "Moose" Dupont. Bobby Clarke's adroit stick work with the puck and on rivals' ankles didn't hurt their reputation any. Then there was the sharp-shooting of Billy Barber, Reggie Leach and Rick MacLeish who strafed goalies with wicked slap shots and whistling wrist shots.

The sellout Spectrum crowd count every game of 17,007 became legend among fans and front offices in the hockey world.

Radio and TV ratings zoomed, PRISM—our premium cable system—was born, jerseys and other merchandise flew off the shelves and sponsors clamored to climb aboard the runaway train. Suddenly, the Flyers were a national craze and a burgeoning money machine.

Most of the players planted roots in the area and could be found after most home games mingling with fans at Rexy's Bar across the Delaware River in Collingswood, New Jersey. The heroes were real, they could be seen and they could be touched.

Ed Snider partied with the players at home, on the road and in the off season. He was with them every step of the way, backing them with deluxe facilities at the Spectrum and training amenities at Penn's Class of '23 rink, upgrading team travel and never failing to hit the home locker room after every game to congratulate or commiserate.

Philly's other pro teams' success couldn't compare to the craze and adulation. The Flyers owned the town. It was the best of times, and it laid the foundation for Ed Snider's ascension to financial success.

But it did even more for Philadelphia. It lifted the city out of its doldrums, gave people something to feel proud about and helped overcome the deep inferiority complex of an underdog city stuck between world capitals New York and Washington, DC.

Coach Freddie "The Fog" Shero, a dotty, professorial type who studied the game, wrote on the locker room blackboard the morning of May 19, 1974, before the crucial game six versus Boston, **"Win today and we walk together forever."**

He couldn't have been more prophetic. Many of the players still live in the area, remain a close-knit group, attend games and even skate in alumni charity games.

As noted earlier, the Flyers chairman, on his deathbed some 40 years later in 2016 and barely able to speak, asked his son, Jay, to tell the world how thankful he was "for what the Flyers did for me and for my family."

With more breath, Ed Snider could have added "and for the city," which two generations later staunchly supports its beloved Flyers, in search of the holy grail—a third Stanley Cup and another boisterous parade.

14

PRISM Dishes It Out
We Help Pioneer Cable TV

It was a Saturday afternoon in winter, 2019 when I sat down to watch TV.

Couldn't decide among 23 college football games—yes, 23! Or the 6 international soccer games, boxing, water polo, track and field or Olympics trials. My 50-inch, 4K smart Sony tantalized me with thousands more choices from Netflix, Hulu, Amazon, Showtime, HBO, NBA, NHL, Fox and God knows what all! Hell, I could even tell my Buck Rogers remote to instantly transport "My Favorites." And, of course, my smart phone was busy "enhancing" scores, odds and in-game statistics.

I don't gamble, so—assuming I could make a choice of options—I could peacefully watch a game without worrying my ass off about covering (where my team wins, but I lose) a plethora of propositions and fantasy league results.

This parfait of endless choices wasn't always the case.

Growing up in our candy store in Brewerytown was the best possible life a kid could have. I just didn't know how lucky I was. My entertainment consisted of radio, newspapers, magazines and comic books. Newspapers, a penny or two each, included the *Inquirer, Bulletin, Daily News, Public Ledger* and *Record*. Batman, Superman, Detective, Spider-Man and those early Stan Lee Marvel comic books, now worth a fortune, were ten cents. For ten bucks, I'd be worth millions now. Who knew?

All this, and going to the Fairmount movie theater four blocks down Girard for a noon Saturday matinee, where for a dime you got a

Pathé newsreel, a Warner Bros. cartoon and an action-packed double feature.

When television burst onto the scene after World War II, we were mesmerized. But, for most of us, the only way we got to see it was to bundle up after dinner and stand outside the Bell Music appliance store a few blocks away and watch one of the three channels available through the plate glass window.

The store owner would leave a TV set running after he closed around 7:00 p.m., and we'd often stand there like idiot lemmings even as the picture began flipping and became unwatchable.

After about 15 minutes of fluttering our eyeballs, we'd go home frustrated. Sets had something called horizontal and vertical control knobs, but there was no one inside the store at night to adjust them.

Back then, television stations signed on about 11:00 a.m. with a test pattern for technicians to fine tune the picture. The first shows would begin about 4:00 p.m., usually with a Western serial episode of Hopalong Cassidy or a really boring British movie where you couldn't understand half their stiff-upper-lip dialogue. Hollywood was boycotting the television "fad" to force people into the theaters, so all we got to watch on TV were foreign films, in crappy black and white, with no closed captions.

There were no TV networks yet, so the local stations went dark around 10:00 p.m. after the "late news." The national anthem was played, we stood and crossed our hearts—and that was that!

The three channels—3, 6 and 10—televised only live, original content until shows began emanating from New York City flagships NBC, ABC and CBS. Soon, more local channels appeared—first Channel 12, an educational channel from Wilmington, Delaware, that all but ignored its home state, beaming programs of interest to its giant market to the north. Then came UHF, an Ultra High Frequency band that fed us channels 17, 29, 48 and, later, 57.

The big networks grew quickly, with RCA's NBC network miraculously giving birth to color TV. Shows began transmitting from Hollywood in 1948 as something called the coaxial cable, an insulated wire physically laid across the country, connected the coasts.

Vaudeville's and radio's Milton Berle was such a huge hit with his NBC Texaco comedy hour at 8:00 p.m. Tuesdays that sales of TV sets—about $200 (nearly $2200 in today's dollars) for a 9-inch RCA, Dumont, Zenith, Sylvania or GE set—went off the charts. The zany comedian is widely credited with almost single-handedly getting TV off the ground. "Uncle Miltie," with his slapstick skits and gaudy get-ups, created such a national craze that entire cities saw mysterious drops in water pressure at the same time every Tuesday night. Turned out that people across the country were holding it in until the show ended and then rushing en masse to relieve themselves.

Things soon became mind-boggling as cable TV was invented--by accident—in Mahanoy City, 86 miles west of Philly.

John Walson, Sr., owner of a Mahanoy store selling radios, was an engineer with a love for electronics. "One of the things that got me interested in going into cable TV in a large way," he said, "were the crowds that gathered in front of my store in 1948. When I first put those three channels on, the street was completely blocked with viewers, people watching the pictures through the window."

Walson, who died in 1993 at age 78, is considered the father of cable TV—although there are competing sources of early cable who might contest that claim. After graduating from Mahanoy Township High School, he entered Loyola University with the intention of becoming a physician. Soon, he rekindled his adolescent interest in electricity. Coyne Electrical School was nearby, and before long he forgot about medicine and enrolled as an engineering student.

Selling early television sets in in his store was difficult, as it was almost impossible to receive clear pictures from the Philadelphia stations so far away and blocked by mountains.

So he erected a basic tower on top of a nearby mountain and strung army surplus, heavy duty wiring along trees down to his appliance store, where customers now saw a sharp picture. But when buyers got their TVs home, all they got was snowy signals, which prompted the resourceful Walson to run wires to their houses directly from either his store or tower. Thus was born CATV, the Community Antenna Television service. Soon, he began charging a small fee for each hookup. Walson's family still operates its cable business, called Service Electric Co., with about 300,000 subscribers.

When we formed PRISM, the Philadelphia Regional In-home Sports & Movies premium network, in 1976, John Walson was one of the first big operators to sign on, giving our fledgling project an immediate injection of industry credibility. Walson was an old, grizzled cable guy by the time I pitched him on PRISM over dinner at Trainer's Restaurant, the now-gone legendary family place in Quakertown in Bucks County.

It was a long night with more than a few drinks, and when he finally signed the agreement to carry PRISM on his cable system, I made a big show of calling a sleepy but elated Ed Snider on my rotary-dial car phone, one of the few mobile units in the area at the time, so the Big Man personally could congratulate and thank Walson.

Service Electric was a big catch. It was a large system and gave us an instant boost, as other cable operators were watching to see if PRISM had any traction.

A few weeks later, I launched a promotional campaign to convince other area cable systems, mostly mom-and-pop operations, to carry our package. The small cable system in suburban Upper Darby had already signed on. Atlantic City came on board next, and others throughout eastern Pennsylvania and southern New Jersey followed. Philly would not be officially wired until later.

Professional sports teams had territorial broadcasting rights that limited the sending of our signal too far into neighboring cities and states. For instance, we couldn't transmit our games past Trenton because it infringed on rights of New York teams. Or too far south into territories of Baltimore or Washington teams.

We were offering Phillies, Flyers and 76ers home games and recent movies, all without any commercials. Plus, we served up anything that played the Spectrum that we produced or could acquire the rights for, including boxing, wrestling, roller derby, indoor track and small local bands. None of the big acts, however, allowed PRISM to show their performances.

My marketing campaign was aimed at cable operators with the teaser slogan, *We Can Dish It Out. Can You Take It?* This showed actual microwave dishes atop the Spectrum, one pointing northwest towards Lehigh County cable firms and the other beaming us into South Jersey. Things were so simple in those days that one of our studio engineers would stand on the roof of the Spectrum while another climbed atop a cable system building miles away in New Jersey or suburban Philly. Each had a strong flashlight, and if they could see one another, it meant that the point-to-point microwave dishes could send a clean signal to the cable system uninterrupted by trees, terrain or buildings.

PRISM came about after the Flyers became wildly popular, with the Bullies taking eastern Pennsylvania and southern New Jersey by storm. The region became hockey-crazed, games were sold out and tickets were hard to come by. I even ran an ad that read: *Hockey Tickets Aren't Sold – They're Inherited.*

Earlier, in 1974, we had experimented by televising Flyers home games over telephone lines into nearby saloons, which, in South Philly, existed on just about every corner. It was an instant success, with bar owners selling "season tickets" for reserved stools. We charged them ten bucks per head monthly based on their legal occupancy numbers. Philadelphia Mayor Jim Kenney, a huge Flyers fan, says as a kid he and friends would walk from their homes near Second Street and sneak into bars on 15th or 16th Streets to catch the games because we weren't sending games to their neighborhood yet.

Anyway, in '76 came the big break in forming PRISM:

We were approached by execs from a consortium of film companies—United Artists, Paramount, Warner Bros. and 20th Century Fox—who asked if we were interested in forming a regional premium TV network. Home Box Office had become powerful and was dictating to Hollywood how much it was willing to pay to run their movies. The film studios believed that creating a spate of regional sports and movie networks would overcome HBO's dominance and create greater revenues for their films—which it did.

The four movie companies and the Spectrum became equal partners in a venture that I named PRISM—remember, one of the definitions of the word "spectrum" is "colors emanating from a prism." Ed Snider asked me to head up the endeavor and committed the Flyers and select Spectrum events as programming content. We convinced the Phillies and 76ers to sell us their home games as well, despite their (unfounded) fears that it would hurt their gates.

PRISM charged the cable operators $10 a month for each of their subscribers who signed up for our programming. The cable operators charged subscribers an average of $12 a month. Of the $10 fee, we paid the Flyers, Phillies, 76ers and movie groups each $2 per subscriber per month and operated the system on the remaining $2 for each subscriber.

We built a modest studio in the basement of the Spectrum, next to the team locker rooms, and at 5:30 p..m., September 1, 1976, I pressed the button to turn us on.

PRISM sportscaster Hugh Gannon announced us to the world (actually, to only six subscribers in neighboring Upper Darby, plus Ed, the security guard in the executive entrance).

"Good evening, everyone. PRISM, the pay television network, is on the air," Gannon intoned.

Following this was our first movie, *The Wind and the Lion*. Movies from our partners followed nonstop, including a Woody Allen film festival, and nine days later we aired our first sports event, the Phillies hosting the Chicago Cubs from Veterans Stadium.

But over the next few months, I noticed while viewing PRISM in my office that dark scenes in movies were almost unwatchable, looking nearly black, whether shot in color or black and white. I checked with some of our cable operators and learned it was the same on their end. HBO's movies were bright and sharp, and we looked second class.

We were running films from basic, three-quarter-inch cassettes in standard VCRs, but what we really needed, I learned, was an expensive upgrade to then state-of-the-art, one-inch tape. That new equipment would cost about $1 million.

I told Ed Snider we had to improve or start losing subscribers. Ed called in our studio engineer, who corroborated my concern, and with trademark decisiveness, he made the call to get it done. He convinced our movie partners to help fund it, and a month later, PRISM movies were right up there in clarity and crispness with those of HBO.

Ed Snider had many admirable business attributes, and doing everything first class was at the very top of his list.

PRISM didn't make a profit in its first five years, but turned the corner bigtime, peaking in the mid-1980s with nearly 375,000 subscribers, each paying PRISM a minimum of $10 per month. (I had left the Snider organization in 1980 to become president of the 76ers.)

By 1984, Snider bought out the movie partners and owned PRISM outright. About that time, it was getting expensive to operate the system, and PRISM, rather than increase prices to cable operators in a down economy, decided to run commercials during sports events, ending a unique benefit for our viewers.

Snider eventually sold PRISM to Cablevision in New York, sat on the sidelines for two years with a non-compete contract clause, and in 1989 launched SportsChannel Philadelphia, which reacquired the Philly sports teams' rights and ultimately drove PRISM off the air.

His staff went on to create similar sports channels in New York, Chicago, New England and other regions, which were renamed Comcast SportsNet in 1996 when the cable giant bought two thirds of Snider's Spectacor holdings, including the Flyers and Wells Fargo Center. Upon Snider's death in 2016, Comcast acquired the remainder of his related assets from his estate. In 2019, Comcast rebranded the sports channels under its NBC Sports umbrella.

So what started out as signing up South Philly bars for thirsty Flyers fans, and some guy in Mahanoy City delivering clear pictures by cable wire, became a multi-billion-dollar business.

I loved being in on the beginning of an industry that revolutionized the world of viewing. And I applaud those who followed and took it to great success.

But I have a problem.

Which of these 23 bleepin' football games am I going to watch?

15

The King's Last Act

Curtains for Elvis

Sweat ran down Elvis Presley's puffy jowls as he labored on the Spectrum stage on this warm and humid evening of May 22, 1977. He wasn't the picture of health, but who could have imagined that 12 weeks later he'd be dead? At age 42?

It was one more concert on another long tour for the King, but for his fevered Philly fans it was a Saturday night for the ages. Nearly 19,000 available seats had been snapped up long ago.

The audience was a mix, fewer enraptured teenagers and more older fans, dressed like you'd do for a Sinatra concert. This was a mega-event. Like seeing royalty.

The evening began with the show's Joe Guerico Orchestra warming up the devoted, expectant crowd, which filled all three levels except for some lower obstructed seats directly behind the stage. Famed gospel singers J. D. Sumner and the Stamps Quartet got things rolling with their energetic revival music, followed by the Sweet Inspirations, an R&B female group founded by Cissy Houston, mother of Whitney Houston.

Veteran comedian Jackie Kahane was next. He was one of Presley's buddies and could do 15 minutes or 45 minutes, depending on the mood of the crowd or how long it was taking Elvis to get it together. More than once, over the years, Jackie was booed off the stage by impatient crowds. Tonight, he delivered about 15 minutes of clean, funny material to an overeager audience. Then came an announcement of intermission, which was not met kindly by the animated crowd. Finally, after a lengthy break, the house lights blinked, the place went dark and the crowd surged to life.

Elvis' entrance music, 2001: A Space Odyssey, filled the air. The backup singers joined in, bringing the throng to its feet with their trio of ascending "AAAHHHs." Drummer Ronnie Tutt pounded the beat, powerful spotlights twirled the building, the orchestra picked up the count and the brass section rattled the rafters.

A flashlight flickers from the bottom of dark steps at stage right. Elvis comes up and the nanosecond a brilliant white beam hits him, the crowd explodes. It's Elvis! A rainbow of spotlights erupt and thousands of popping flashbulbs strobe the smokey arena. The standing ovation is long, thunderous and punctuated with female shrieks.

He apologized for being a little late, alibiing that he had got lost in the parking lot. Some girls near the stage laughed loudly. He looked at them and said, "I'm not kidding you . . . but I am lying to you."

From my viewpoint seated with a date a few rows from the stage, his dissipated condition was obvious, though hardly cardiac-arrest fatal. Bloated, short of breath and backed by the orchestra and a small band, plus two sets of singers to mask his hoarseness, it was like watching a god fade away in slow motion.

Out of Tupelo, Mississippi, he burst onto the scene in 1954 at age 19. Two years later, he was an international phenomenon with that sultry hip-twitching style that both shocked and titillated America. Booked on the Ed Sullivan variety show on CBS TV, the cameras would show him only from the waist up so as not to shock the nation's sensibilities.

Elvis had a history in Philadelphia even before playing the Spectrum for five shows on four tours between 1971 and 1977. Pandemonium had set in when he came to the staid Quaker City in 1957 to play four shows in two days at the old Arena at 46th and Market Streets. With long, slicked-back hair, heavy sideburns and Hollywood looks like Travolta's later Danny Zucko, the craze was full on. Philly deejay Bob Menefee called him "Pelvis Pretzel." His fans called him a sensation.

Two decades later, up on the Spectrum stage, his voice had mellowed. More baritone, less range, and sometimes we couldn't even hear him over his assortment of backups. But it mattered not to his faithful, or those seeing him live for the first time. It was another memorable performance by one of the most significant cultural icons of the twentieth century.

He was wearing a white jumpsuit with a large Mexican sundial medallion on the front. It hardly hid the fact that he had become beefy. I remember Elvis clowning a bit and having fun with the audience, picking up roses and small stuffed animals tossed from the crowd and mopping his brow or kissing at least a dozen scarves and lofting them to female fans down front.

One song ended with his fingers outstretched and a thumb near his mouth. He contemplated his thumb for a few seconds, then playfully popped it into his mouth and suckled it like a baby. The audience cracked up. At one point, he turned and acknowledged the fans in the second and third levels behind the stage. He took his time thanking them as he was bathed in a blizzard of camera flashes.

One classic hit followed another: "See, See Rider" . . . "I Got a Woman" . . . "Love Me Tender" . . . "Jailhouse Rock" . . . "You Gave Me a Mountain" . . . "Now or Never" . . . and on and on for about 75 minutes. At one point, he said he was going to sing "My Way" but didn't know the words and would have to fake it. An alert aide handed him a piece of paper with the words, and, of course, he killed it.

After a rip-roaring "Hound Dog," he told the crowd we were great and "we'll be glad to come back up here." By this point, his top was unbuttoned, and his chest was soaked in sweat. He said not to pay attention to what we read or hear about him, saying, "I'm in good health and really love performing."

"Let's take it home," he cued the musicians, and launched into a rousing "Can't Help Falling in Love," with an ending so powerful that it had everyone standing and cheering.

Then, he was gone. No one moved. We just sat there. Drained.

Elvis indeed, had left the building.

16

The Comeback Kid

Reunited . . . and It Feels So Good

It's a warm, rainy Sunday morning in June 2008, and I'm heavily into the *Inquirer* comics section when my home phone rings. My wife, Vicky, is sitting next to me in the family room and our three young kids are somewhere around the house. She answers, says a few friendly words into the phone and hands it to me.

"It's Ed Snider," she says, looking at me wide-eyed.

"What!?"

I hadn't spoken with or seen Ed much since I had left his organization in 1980—28 years prior! He's calling from his mansion in Montecito, California, near Santa Barbara, where it's gotta be, what, not even 8:00 a.m.

After brief pleasantries, he asks, "Did they call you?"

"Who?"

"My guys from Comcast Spectacor. I told them to call you and hire you back . . . to close the Spectrum."

I reply calmly that I haven't heard from anyone, but I'm about to shit myself.

"I want you to come back and give the building a proper sendoff," he says. "No one cares more for that building than you—you're the perfect guy to do it."

I explain I'm already working on a project in Reno, Nevada, overseeing construction of a $60 million stadium and staffing a new Triple A baseball team, and that I travel to Nevada every other week.

"So," he persists, "you'll work for me every other week when you're in Philly."

I thank him, promise to call his guys from Reno the next day and hang up.

This is awesome, I'm thinking, my mind racing so hard that I suddenly have no interest in Garry Trudeau's "Doonesbury"—or tackling the big Sunday crossword puzzle.

For three years, I had been home on my butt, looking for an opportunity. Only five weeks earlier, the Reno project had popped up. My friend, Jerry Katzoff, had called me for advice on the marketing of suites in a stadium he was about to build for the top farm team of the Arizona Diamondbacks.

I met Jerry for a quick lunch in the Latham Hotel on Rittenhouse Square and offered him a bunch of ideas. He was in town to see his dentist and was flying to Los Angeles in a few hours. Jerry's a big-time developer who owns a string of upscale *Il Mulino* restaurants and a famed spa in Texas called *The Green House* and has homes all over the place. His Bucks County manse originally was owned by William Penn. He has a condo in Manhattan, a getaway in Maine and a house in Santa Barbara, near Ed Snider's. He's a sharp attorney with a genuine easy demeanor.

"Would you be willing to come to Reno to take a look at the project?" he asked. It's a big, exciting opportunity and he's a fun, generous guy, so I glance at my empty schedule and advise him I can squeeze it in.

Two days later at dinner in a casino in "the Biggest Little City in the World," with Jerry and his son, Stuart, his 30-something partner, whom I've known since he was a baby, I make a deal to spend every other week working in Reno. Jerry's a class act and puts me up in a lavish suite at the huge Grand Sierra Resort & Casino, agrees to pay all my expenses and urges me to fly my family out a couple of times. I love this oddly charming Vegas town and absolutely looked forward to rising at 3:00 a.m. every other Monday to catch the 6:10 a.m. flight to Reno. There were no direct flights from Philly, and with a long layover in Chicago or Dallas, it took me 11 hours door-to-door to make the trip.

Now, the Spectrum job falls in my lap.

Holy crap! Going from no job to two great new ones not only will do wonders for my aching bank account—but for my marriage. Vicky, who's 20 years younger than I, likes to say that she married me "for better or worse—but not for lunch!" Being home and unproductive day in and day out with this lively, elegant beauty and our kids, Alexandra, then 17, Matthew, 14, and Caroline, 11, had been a strain. Vicky, of course, is my second wife and I couldn't afford to lose this one. She's a solid partner and a wonderful mom, not to mention a head turner.

So, on my layover Monday morning at bustling O'Hare in Chicago, I call Snider's right-hand guy, Peter Luukko, negotiate a deal, and agree to start work on the Spectrum the following Monday. Thus begins a whirlwind of activity, juggling two fantastic jobs—2,654 miles apart.

Walking into the spacious Wells Fargo Center on my first day in June 2008 was an eye opener. The business and the facilities had changed from my days at the cozy Spectrum. Everything was bigger, more formal and totally more corporate.

Amazingly, Gloria in the parking lot booth and Ed at the front desk were still around from my Spectrum days and welcomed me warmly.

"I heard you're back," the old security guard said with a big smile. He phoned ahead Snider's office for permission to let me in, unlocked a set of thick glass doors to the executive elevator, swiped his key card to activate it and pressed the button to the third-floor offices.

The steel doors closed with a hushed snick, and as the well-appointed car started, I threw a left-right-left Rocky combo and danced like I'm at the top of the art museum steps.

"Yeah, mother fuckers, I'm baaack!" I exulted.

Ed's marvelous secretary AnneMarie—excuse me, administrative assistant—also an old Spectrum friend, met me at the elevator and walked me down the mahogany-paneled foyer to executive offices like you'd find in a staid, established Philadelphia law firm. The hall is lined with interior-lit glass cases containing significant memorabilia like Charles Barkley's giant sneakers, Bobby Clarke's MVP trophy, a signed 76ers basketball and assorted Flyers awards and mini–Stanley Cups.

Ed Snider had asked me to see him as soon as I arrived to give me my marching orders.

"Mr. Snider's on the phone," she said. In the meantime, would I like fresh-brewed Columbian coffee, herbal tea, hot chocolate, designer water, cookies or finger pastries from the break alcove behind her desk while waiting? I stroll over and see a shelf holding jars of gluten-free stuff like sugar-free and organic candies, free-range pretzels, natural juices, locally sourced chips, sustainable popcorn and other exotic Whole Foods specialties on which to munch. I exaggerate a bit here, but the candy store in which I grew up didn't have an array this grand. We lived on gluten-rich TastyKakes, sugar rock candy and unwrapped licorice sticks.

Ed got off his call and buzzed AnneMarie, who sent me into his grand office, which had a massive, curved glass wall overlooking the parking lot and beyond, across Broad Street and into Roosevelt Park. In a few months, Ed was to move to even grander digs in a spacious corner office on the penthouse level on the opposite, east side of the building from which he could gaze upon the Spectrum, center city, Lincoln Financial Field and Citizens Bank Park.

This day, behind his desk sat built-in shelves displaying awards, trophies and Flyers and family photographs. Near his desk was a soaring model of his Gulfstream 5 jet with the Flyers logo on its tail. On his desk sat a couple of neat piles of correspondence, memos and documents to be reviewed, signed, filed or tossed.

There was a cellphone with the vanity-important last four digits xxx-xxx-6000, but no laptop. Ed never got around to using a computer, but eventually did enjoy the wonders of an iPad propped eye-level on a stand to his right.

Front and center on his polished desk sat a to-do list prepared daily for him by AnneMarie. Down the left side were phone calls to be returned, and pressing items in the middle, which he carefully crossed off in blue ballpoint ink as the day evolved. The right side was for any brief notes to be added.

In the office, Ed preferred a basic Paper Mate or Flair ballpoint or felt pen. Outside, he carried an expensive fountain pen clipped to the inside pocket of his tailored suit jacket. Ed had sartorial class and an understated style, favoring fine wool, midnight blue $5,000 Brioni bespoke suits, and sedate Hermes ties and socks with handmade Italian leather shoes. Trim, tall—and toned, thanks to years with a personal trainer, who visited his office and homes— he cut an elegant figure entering any room.

Ed never was an early riser, usually arriving at the office after 10:00 a.m., but now able to check emails and texts at home and handle calls via Bluetooth speaker in his bullet of a car, a four-door Porsche Panamera. First thing he did in the office was scour the *Inquirer, Daily News* or *USA Today* over coffee in a china cup and a pastry or cake. He read the sports sections first, and if there was something that he didn't like or wanted to follow up, he made a note on his pad. He also reviewed a daily stack of news items mentioning the Flyers or Comcast Spectacor culled and copied by his PR staff from area and national publications.

Ed wasn't shy about calling editors, writers or talk show hosts to let them know he didn't appreciate a particular unfavorable mention of him or of his beloved Flyers. If the papers ran an unflattering photo,

Ed would have his PR staff send one he liked, requesting it be used in the future.

After making or returning the most important calls, he would go over his mail, paying close attention to negative letters. He would dictate straightforward responses stating why he disagreed or agreed with the writer's view. He especially enjoyed answering letters from intelligent fans. Complaints about arena service, whether parking, seating or game experience were referred to department heads for prompt handling—and to get back to him with their follow-up. His attention to detail knew no bounds and was one of the bedrocks of his success.

If he didn't have a lunch meeting out of the office, he liked to eat a meal at his desk, prepared by one of the building's restaurant chefs. Due to celiac disease, he was a finicky eater, avoiding bread as much as possible, other than an occasional, must-have Nick's roast beef sandwich. A favorite lunch would be a hot roast turkey or chicken platter with stuffing.

Catered lunches for meetings in the conference room a few steps from his office were luscious feasts, including jumbo shrimp or lump crabmeat, salads, roast chicken or beef filet slices, poached or broiled fish, a green vegetable and pasta. Oh, and, of course, lox and bagels and fresh Jewish corned beef and pastrami delivered from Hymie's Delicatessen on the Main Line.

■ ■ ■

Ed remains seated behind his desk as I enter, smiles warmly, and gives me a quick rundown on the lay of the land.

"Lou, my guys could care less about the Spectrum," he says. "I want you to use your creativity and ideas to honor it—like nobody but you can. Just do what you think best and if anyone gives you trouble, throw my name around."

Wow, like the Ed I knew and loved. Just get it done! That was it. That was him.

Oh, one more thing, he remembers, as I start to leave.

"Look, Lou," he says very seriously, "It's not like the old days. They have this department called HR, Human Relations. You got to be very careful with the staff. There's no messing around."

Even in 2008, years before #MeToo, it was quite clear to me that the anything-goes "Mad Men" days of office carousing not only were dead—but buried.

"Don't worry," I tell him, pausing for effect. "Any girl hits on me, I'm reporting it immediately."

Ed cracks up, but gives me a nervous smile as if to hammer home the seriousness of it.

Turns out it was no problem. The female staff, mostly about age 24, were intelligent, confident professionals who not only had never heard of me, but could care less about a 72-year-old, gray-haired geezer in their midst.

The office atmosphere in the sprawling Wells Fargo Center was Comcast-corporate to the max, quiet, almost funereal. Both execs and staff spoke in hushed tones. It was like a library or insurance company with scores of worker bees in endless cubicles or seated at rows of desks clicking away beneath computer screens or speaking softly into their work phones. Rarely did I see anyone on their cell phone.

I will say that the staff was well trained and competent, and the entire organization was run quite efficiently by the popular and affable Comcast Spectacor president Peter Luukko.

As the younger employees learned of my role in the dark ages of the Flyers, Spectrum, PRISM and Spectacor, many introduced themselves reverentially, offering to help me in any way they could.

I was shown to my new office on the executive level, an upper floor of a recently added wing with large windows facing Lincoln Financial Field. All the handsome offices along this city block–long wall housed department vice presidents, directors and their support staffs. Within minutes, I received a visit from an IT rep, who set up my company PC, hooked me into the internal and internet networks and patched in a color printer. Did I need a company laptop, cell phone, beeper or any other electronic gadgetry? All I had to do was ask, he said. Word got around fast that I was Chairman Snider's guy. All this attention was quite an eye-opener, but no thank you, I brought my own laptop and cell phone and didn't want a beeper.

I also learned that there was plenty of other help at my fingertips, including graphic arts, to create marketing materials, TV-radio production to make Spectrum commercials of short videos and social media departments to reach the more than 500,000 data base of Comcast Spectacor customers and followers. What's more, my position permitted me to buy a small amount of Comcast stock each month at a 15-percent discount of current share price and, as a "Comcast Insider," my monthly home Comcast bill was discounted from over $250 to about $60. I was issued a company credit card and reimbursed for auto and out-of-pocket business expenses.

First thing I experienced was meetings, lots of meetings, almost daily. Most of them, deliciously catered.

There was a weekly meeting to review the week's past and upcoming games and events, for event personnel. Another weekly meeting was for reports from about 15 departments. Then, there was a monthly meeting where vice presidents reported progress and issues on their projects. Ed had his own regular meetings with his "Office of the Chairman" top aides. I also chaired my own regular meetings on closing the Spectrum, discussing bookings or creating new events, creating memorabilia, promotions, tributes and demolition ceremonies.

Ed Snider had made it quite clear to his brass that the Spectrum project was a personal priority and that he wanted it done in a first-class manner. This made my job much easier, and I was eagerly welcomed by most everyone involved.

There was one brief exception, a middle-aged female vice president who resisted some of my initiatives on celebrating the final year of my beloved building. She had a full plate of other responsibilities and may have been stretched too thin by adding one more project—mine.

Her job included keeping the building fresh and bright, overseeing maintenance and improvements, office furnishings, personnel logistics, 76ers and Flyers game-day decorations and holiday festivities. She also was charged with moving and integrating scores of Spectrum workers into the Wells Fargo Center offices.

After a second incident with her at one of my meetings, I visited her office for a chat. She had a strong personality and an impressive background in big company governance, which I respected, but I couldn't allow her to tell me publicly how to do my job.

After a quick hello, I got right to it.

"Gail, what do you think your role is on the Spectrum project?"

"To help you," she said, quickly getting the tenor of the conversation.

"Good," I said evenly. "Then we will have no problem."

After that, Gail Clark and I got along just great. She pitched in enthusiastically and we became tight friends, the odd couple working together on my project—while I advised her on some of hers. We spent so much time together, eating lunch in the company cafeteria and hanging in each other's offices, that I started calling her my O.W., Office Wife, and still do to this day when we're in touch. Gail was a gem and I miss working with her.

It was great to be back again with Ed Snider, but he was a much different guy now, light years from the days when we hung out without restraint. Much more serious, more corporate and all business.

His pals were billionaires, governors and senators, big-name stars and bold-letter items on both coasts. That old spontaneous, fun side appeared only in private, and not often.

We would meet in his office a couple times a week for updates on projects or just to shoot the shit. He would ask my take on some of his execs and to quietly look into certain things in the organization that he didn't want to involve his staff in, like why were certain things taking so long, or who was sitting on it. I'd give him my frank opinion, but mostly let him know I wasn't his spy, and he'd admit, "You're right, I shouldn't put you in that position."

"Call the guy in and just ask him," I'd say.

We covered a wide range of topics from people to politics to ladies. Once we talked about mortality, our ages and mental acuity.

"How long can you keep doing this?" I asked. Comcast Spectacor also owned the 76ers at the time and he was attending almost every game for both teams.

"I've got to pace myself," he'd say, while recognizing that it was important to be seen in his very visible courtside basketball seats as well as in his Flyers suite.

"As long as I can stay sharp, I'll stay on," he said. "If I feel myself slipping, I'll call it quits."

"You've still got it," he said, "Still on the ball, just like when we were younger."

Then he added wistfully, "Sadly, Lou, you and I are on the five-yard-line."

He meant that the end zone loomed. I preferred to believe I was about to score.

He'd be stiff at first when I met with him, but usually would ease up after I brought up a few anecdotes of how we used to live it up. That would get him relaxed and the old Eddie came out.

I remember running into him many years before at a club in center city after I'd left the organization. "We're not having as much fun without you—but we're better organized," he said. Was that supposed to be a compliment?

By now, he had a $50-million mansion in California, a family compound in Maine, multi-million dollar condos in New York City and Philly, a home in suburban Gladwyne, art worth nearly $10 million, a fortune in Comcast stock, a driver and a private jet. He loved fast cars and had, among other luxury rides, a McLaren at his California estate probably worth over $250,000.

His mind always was in high gear. When not on the Flyers, it focused on civic, philanthropic or conservative causes, especially on national politics, where he considered then President Obama the enemy.

Closing the Spectrum was my job—but keeping it open was my personal mission. I reached out to a few connected friends to see whether they had a use for the building: sports museum, small event venue, movie or TV sound stage.

I thought I got lucky right away when a friend, Sharon Pinkenson, head of the Greater Philadelphia Film Office, told me there was a strong need for television and movie production facilities here. The Spectrum could be perfect, she said. It's big enough to stage scenes at one end and produce sets at the other.

The state was offering enticing film credits then for shows produced here and, importantly, it cost a lot less to produce shows here than most other East Coast locations. "My building" already had a restaurant for the crews, dressing rooms for the cast and plenty of parking, and it was close to talent from New York and within minutes of the Amtrak Metroliner and Philly International Airport.

Reps working on a pilot for a proposed NBC show about a high-profile DC lawyer who loved hockey visited the building, liked what they found and wanted to shoot it here. If the show got picked up, it could mean years of significant rent for Spectacor, other productions of movies, TV and radio commercials, documentaries and basically a new lease on life for the building.

I started working with Luukko's execs to try to make it a reality. They said they would handle the negotiations. But when producers flew in from Hollywood to make a deal, our guys laid stiff terms on them that made it impossible for them to rent the building. This pissed off the visitors who, based on my enthusiastic reception, thought a reasonable deal already was in the works.

I quickly realized that there was little interest in saving the building, despite their boss's passion for the venue. I stifled a gut urge to get Ed Snider involved because I didn't want to go over the execs' heads and be poisoned as his "eyes and ears." I had made up my mind before coming back that I was not getting involved in office politics or Snider family matters, both fraught with land mines that had blown me up many years before. So that promising Spectrum lifeline went as quickly as it came.

I threw myself into taking the building apart, literally brick by brick, and selling its pieces. My interns photographed and catalogued every item I thought we could sell, from signage, artwork, seats, basketball floorboards and hoops, hockey dasher boards and glass, goalie nets and concert posters to locker room stalls. I even had wallpaper with giant graphics of circus and ice shows and Stanley Cup Parades peeled off to sell.

None of this would have been possible without total support from my "O.W." and the building's classy operations staff, who got into it and willingly worked with me to pay homage to the Spectrum. Many of the carpenters, plumbers and electricians had kept the old building up and running with duct tape, baling wire and bandages for years. They knew every inch of the building and were eager to help give it an honorable sendoff. I had been a popular chief of the Spectrum and Flyers with great relationships with the union tradespeople and "back of the house" staff and found it no different this time around.

I learned long ago that if you treated people with respect and asked for their help instead of ordering them around or sending blunt memos, they would see it as a team effort and eagerly pitch in. It didn't hurt, of course, that they knew I had a direct line to the chairman's office.

Often, as we walked through the building or at an event, I would introduce Ed to one of the workers he didn't know and praise their support of the Spectrum project. The boss loved it and the workers couldn't wait to spread word of "Mr. Snider" shaking their hands in appreciation.

I took calls from companies looking to buy the giant ceiling speakers, pulleys and scene winches, even several hundred gallons of the chemical glycol, which ran though pipes embedded in the hockey floor that kept the ice cold. Others wanted seats they had actually sat in at Flyers or 76ers games, which one of our execs suggested I not waste my time on. But the operations guys thought it was a cool idea, and among the thousands of fixed seats we sold at $395 per pair, we located dozens of the exact seats for nostalgic season-ticket holders.

One Flyers fan asked to buy her single seat tucked next to the stairs in the third level. But when she arrived inside the Spectrum to pick it up, there was a problem with the seat we brought down.

"That's not my chair," she said to me, upset. How could she tell?

"Because I scratched my initials under the seat with a nail clipper at the last game we had," she said.

Sure enough, the red metal bottom had no such marking.

One of the workers tried to talk her into taking it anyway, as it had been hauled all the way down from the top of the third level and there was a line of customers waiting behind her to pick up their seats. She shook her head, disappointed, and lingered nearby while we tended to other fans who were in awe not only to be standing on the hallowed floor of their Spectrum, but to be allowed to drive their cars directly down the tunnel and onto the concrete floor to pick up their chairs. Some of the fans, looking up at the stands and scoreboard, couldn't believe the view. They'd never seen it the way Wilt, Moses Malone, Dave Schultz and Billy Barber had. By this time, about half the 17,500 seats had been removed and there was debris and construction equipment cluttering the stands.

All of a sudden, the woman was back.

"I found it," she said. "My seat's still up there! It's got my initials on it."

Somehow, without being spotted, this determined young lady picked her way three levels up over littered, obstructed steps, like a rock climber, to the top level and found her personal perch from which she had enjoyed so many Flyers games. Thank God a safety compliance officer wasn't on the scene.

You know by now what came next. I dispatched two workers to traipse her dangerous trail and bring that dang thing down. Sure enough, there were her initials etched into the metal cushion pan.

That's the kind of sendoff I wanted to give the Spectrum, a building known far and wide by millions for hockey and basketball, boxing and wrestling, roller derby and tennis, circus, ice shows and its vaunted music sound.

We sold more than 5,000 bricks, 4,500 seats and a thousand other various treasured items, including two urinals from the locker rooms. Yes, urinals. Toilets used by their heroes. Hey, who wouldn't want something the 76ers' Darryl Dawkins or Flyer Moose Dupont pissed in?

One was purchased by a New Jersey woman who said she was redoing her husband's medical office and wanted to surprise him when it was all finished. I don't remember whether he was a hockey or 76ers fan. Might have been a urologist with a bad bladder.

The other one was purchased by a fan for his garage man cave. "That's where I watch all the games," he told me. "I have a big TV, wet bar, stadium seats, stove and fridge. Now, all I need is a urinal and I never have to leave during a game."

The amused building plumber not only had carefully removed the two urinals, but made sure to include all the hardware fittings and piping necessary for the buyers to have them installed so they might work.

We came up with some other great items that sold out quickly.

Sections of the 76ers basketball floor, four by eight feet and weighing 250 pounds, went for $850 each, and I sold dozens of them. We cut up smaller pieces and mounted them on commemorative plaques small and large, which were gobbled up as well.

One guy, a New York Wall Street exec, made a wedding gift for his daughter of a post-ceremony dance floor comprising nine sections of the Spectrum basketball floor used in the 1982 March Madness NCAA semifinals. The bride-to-be was a crazy Duke fan and idolized Christian Laettner, who made one of sport's most historic buzzer beaters as the Blue Devils shocked Kentucky at the Spectrum and went on to win the national championship.

We marked the exact spot from which Laettner launched his fabled, last-second shot, shipped it to a country club in North Carolina to be assembled as a section that had covered from under the Spectrum basket to beyond the foul line and happily deposited the buyer's payment to the amount of $10,700, plus delivery costs.

The loving dad said he was going to tell her what it represented as he whirled her onto the polished maple floor for the traditional father-daughter dance. I suggested if he really wanted to surprise her, he should get Laettner in the flesh to escort her onto the floor, but maybe that was a bit much—especially for the poor groom. The dad promised me a video, but none ever came.

I had the staff save barrels of melted Spectrum ice from the last American Hockey League Philadelphia Phantoms game at the building and shipped them to a firm in Chicago where the liquid was condensed into permanent crystals, mixed with plastic bits and encased into Flyers "Spectrum Ice" coasters. Keep one in your freezer, set your beer or soda on it and your favorite beverage stays cold for hours! We sold thousands of these until we ran out of "Spectrum juice."

Another big hit were plaques made from the hockey glass containing etched signatures of every player on the two Stanley Cup Championship teams. We priced them at $74.75 and they sold out immediately. We restocked and sold out again, this time at $125 each. What really was fulfilling were the heartfelt stories from fans purchasing memorabilia on our Remember the Spectrum website or at concession stands—like the woman who bought a pair of seats for her dad, an original season Flyers ticket holder. We located the seats he had sat in for 40-plus years and shipped them to his home in Florida, where he moved after retiring.

"He sits in them for every Flyers game he can get on TV down there," she said, "He's so happy, he cries." Wow! If that doesn't tug at your heart.

So many people had warm, wonderful stories about their first game, first date, first concert. Or meeting their future mate. A prominent Philadelphia journalist who covers the restaurant scene purchased a framed, vintage Spectrum Ice Capades poster as a gift for his wife, who had spoken for years of the magic of going to the show as a child. Former players and their wives, concert performers and ex-Spectrum executives reached out to me for items that were dear to them from their days in the building.

I loved accommodating as many requests as I could and, for the most part, had terrific support from the staff in making it happen. Some kept telling me I shouldn't be going to all that trouble. But I was hired to do a job, and I damn well was going to do it the way I always have: full tilt.

For the people who worked the building, for the fans who occupied those seats and for the incredible ride it afforded me.

I named it, helped design it, and lived it.

I opened it. And I closed it.

If it were a movie, I'd be inside, drunk, crazed and laughing maniacally.

"Bring on that fucking wrecking crane, you soulless dicks!"

You don't know the half of it. We had a ball and you missed it all.

Ed Snider brought me back for a good reason.

I loved the Spectrum—and he knew I'd do right by it.

I like to think I did.

17

Inside Ed Snider

My Life with the Silver Fox

One by one, they bade goodbye.

Family, friends, corporate titans and sports figures stepped up to the lectern to praise Edward Malcolm Snider, AKA the Silver Fox.

Each spoke of their close relationship with the sports and entertainment firebrand, some poignant, some humorous and some bringing tears from the hushed crowd in his palace of an arena.

Ed Snider had passed away ten days earlier at his estate in California, three months past his 83rd birthday. His casket was brought home by private jet to be interred at West Laurel Hill Cemetery, just outside Philadelphia in Lower Merion Township. He had spent the final years doing everything worldly possible to beat back invasive bladder cancer, but it was one battle he was destined to lose.

Expensive, emerging treatments performed in world-class cancer centers in Switzerland, Philadelphia, New York and Los Angeles served only to forestall the inevitable. Ed's team of top cancer specialists and nurses hovered over him in his mansion in Montecito, an opulent enclave in Santa Barbara, California, but could not control the spreading disease—or the debilitating pain. A helicopter ferried him regularly from his estate to a Los Angeles cancer center to avoid enervating two-hour-plus trips by car.

As time dwindled, I called his cell phone to hear his voice. He didn't answer, but called me right back.

"Lou," he began, in a voice I hardly recognized—tired, even resigned, "I'm not returning many calls these days, but I'm glad to hear from you."

131

I asked how he felt, and he replied, "Pretty bad."

I told him we missed him and hoped he'd be back for the upcoming playoffs.

"I'm not gonna make it," he said.

These were chilling words, the tone clearly indicating he was talking about more than just the playoffs.

"Ed, you've beaten the odds all your life," I said, offering an encouraging response. "And you can beat this, too."

"I'm afraid not," he said. "not this time."

We talked a few minutes more, of good times gone by, and he perked up a bit. Reluctantly, we said our goodbyes. I knew it was the last time I would hear his voice.

I hung up and bawled like a baby.

A few weeks later, with the end in sight, a drained Ed Snider hosted Rabbi Marvin Hier, founder and dean of the Los Angeles–based Wiesenthal Center, which Snider had helped fund to fight anti-Semitism. He was feeling wistful. The rabbi, admiring Ed's library with its glittering awards and symbols of the entrepreneur's vast accomplishments, remarked, "Ed, you've had a good life."

Ed, sighing, took in the room, nodded and agreed. "Yes, I have had a fabulous life . . . a fabulous life."

He was ready. Within weeks, he was on life support. Following anguished discussions, the reeling family agreed to shut down the machines.

No one beats Father Time, but Ed, a street fighter, went down swinging, lasting an amazing eight more days before taking that final breath.

More than 3,000 people, including dozens of members of Flyers teams past and present, had come to witness the elaborate memorial in the vast Wells Fargo Center, home to his treasured franchise and where he had gained most of his incredible wealth, publicly estimated at $2.5 billion. His worth, of course, could not be measured in dollars.

The 90-minute observance was elegant and tasteful. The skating surface had been covered with the black insulated wooden floor used for concerts and the basketball court. But the center ice circle was left open and illuminated, dramatically exposing the Flyers' famous logo and its founder's initials: "EMS." The stage was adorned with Ed's classic look, similar to his favored array of white Dendrobium orchids, David Austin roses and Casablanca lilies that had cheered the invitation-only reception for close friends and family at the Union League a few days earlier.

At that 155-year-old Republican bastion in center city, the family spoke briefly and invited guests to offer personal comments. Daughter Serena and former Flyer Joe Watson offered warm remembrances.

Then, I stepped up to the dais. I first mentioned an example showing a particular trait that made Ed such an effective leader.

"Ed got it," I began. "He was trained in finance but understood a lot more than numbers. He had the uncanny ability to read people and, more importantly, relate to the fans.

"At a meeting about sending ticket invoices in our early days," I continued, "Ed asked why the Flyers box office didn't allow season ticket holders to pay in installments instead of one full remittance.

"When the manager explained that it caused extra work for the ticket office, Ed quickly shot him down. 'I don't care if it's extra work for you, I want it easier for them. They're paying your salary.'

"That was music to my ears and after the meeting, I said, 'Ed, I could've kissed you for that.'" A week later, invoices went out offering payment options—at no interest.

"You see, Ed got it," I said. "He understood business *and* people, a rare trait." I had another story about Ed, this one showing his sense of humor, which few outsiders ever saw.

"Following a Flyers game one night at the Wells Fargo Center, we repaired to the Directors' Lounge for drinks while the parking lot emptied. Comcast Spectacor owned the 76ers at the time and the team was playing the Pistons in Detroit. Ed asked the lounge's long-time major domo, Clayton Sheldon, to switch to the game on the bank of newly installed screens.

"Clayton, unfamiliar with the new remotes, couldn't find the right channel. Ed took the remote, but he too failed. Jack Williams, then president of Comcast SportsNet, grabbed the remote but he, too, failed to navigate the battalion of buttons.

"I'm sitting with my wife, Vicky, watching the curious scene unfold. She leans over to me and says, 'How many CEOs does it take to change a channel?'

"Just then, who walks in but Brian Roberts, the Grand Poohbah of all things cable. Ed says, 'Brian, can you change the channel?' Brian, chairman and CEO of Comcast, takes the remote and as he walks over to the TV, Ed comes over to Vicky and me and whispers:

"'See, you call Comcast—and they send somebody *right over!*'"

Boom! It got a huge laugh and loud applause from those attending the private ceremony, lightening the low-key atmosphere. Did Mister Roberts master the remote? I'll never tell, though it looked like he enjoyed the story, standing about 30 feet in front of me and smiling.

At the arena memorial, the huge building was darkened except for the ice circle and the stage at the west end. It was a fitting setting for the strong-willed and detail-conscious Snider, who owned and operated the team and the now-gone Spectrum with meticulous style and class for more than a half century.

His daughter, Lindy, a gifted speaker, recalled how she and her siblings grew up in her Dad's old Spectrum, roaming the bowels of the arena and meeting the stars. Lindy recounted the night he discovered her secret relationship with Flyers player Kenny "The Rat" Linesman, who was seated a row in front of me in the audience.

"One night after a date we come to the house and we suddenly, shockingly see my dad at the top of the driveway where Kenny would drop me off. We thought he didn't know we were dating. He marches up to the car and he looks at Kenny through the glass and he says, 'Get out!'

"Kenny just sat there looking stricken.

"Dad says again, 'Get out! Come in for a drink. I'm a father first and I'm a boss second.'"

Her brother, Jay, fought tears as he repeated the last full sentence his dad had uttered to him with great effort, one word at a time. Jay said his father asked him to please tell everyone: "'I can't thank . . . the Flyers enough . . . for all they've given . . . to me and my family.'"

Gary Bettman, president of the National Hockey League, admiringly described Ed's fierce competitiveness. He told how the irate owner sent a security car, with flashing lights yet, to stop his car from exiting after a Flyers loss at the Wells Fargo Center and escorted him back to face Ed's wrath. "Mr. Snider wants to see you. Now!" Bettman quoted the guard. He had hoped to make a quick exit with his wife and three kids.

It was a key playoff game that the less talented New York Rangers "stole from the Flyers," Bettman explained, with a clutching, hooking and grabbing plan that the refs for the most part ignored. An infuriated Snider was waiting for him in the lobby. "Do you really want your games played like that?" the steamed owner demanded. Bettman said it was about 20 minutes before he could answer "because there was a fair amount of animated gesticulation going on, none of it by me." Bettman said his family watched the scene through the lobby window.

I wasn't sure whether they were horrified or amused—probably both."

By the time Snider was finished with him, Bettman said the parking lot was empty. As the family finally got back to their car, a drunk fan flung himself across their hood, dousing them with beer. "It was," recalled Bettman, "a fragrant ride home."

The NHL boss said Snider later told him it had to be someone from New York, because no Flyers fan would act like that.

Comcast chairman Brian Roberts, Snider's partner for the previous 20 years, said neither had been certain how their relationship would play out when they joined forces in 1996, so they wrote in a put-sell option to buy one another out after the first year.

It wasn't necessary, Roberts said, because Ed turned out to be "the perfect partner." Roberts said Snider was a great listener, and as they grew closer, Ed sagely urged that Comcast move more aggressively into sports and entertainment content, which, Roberts acknowledged, resulted in the cable company eventually acquiring NBC Universal and locking up long-term rights to the Olympics.

Flyers all-time great Bob Clarke wistfully recalled how Snider taught him some tough love. The team, Clarke, said, was coming off two Stanley Cup championships and facing Montreal in the finals in 1976, as beloved teammate Barry Ashbee withered away from leukemia. The Flyers were swept in four straight—an utter humiliation for this proud bunch of Philly skaters.

"After the funeral [for Ashbee], something was wrong," Clarke said. "I didn't know what it was. I went and sought him [Snider] out. Sat down and said to him, 'For us as players, we stunk. We were fighting to make hockey important when Barry was dying.'"

"And he said in a fatherly voice, 'If you think about it properly, you were still able to play hockey. You probably should have been thankful for that, taken advantage of that. To use Barry's dying as an excuse for not playing well, it's like blaming Barry. And I know you wouldn't want to do that. And certainly, Barry wouldn't want you to do that,'" Clarke recalled Snider telling him.

"It cleared up a lot of unknown thoughts. Once I heard that I thought right away, that's absolutely right. We didn't want to blame Barry for us losing. And we didn't want to use Barry as an excuse, but we did. Which was very, very wrong. And very unfair to Barry," Clarke added.

"I think it was one of those life lessons that you learn from a man like that. It was important in a lot of the decisions I made later in life. You can find excuses if you look for them. There's never a reason to point blame."

Listening to the franchise's greatest player, I thought back to the first time I met Ed Snider. I thought he was your typical business sharpie, what with the black, horn-rimmed glasses, tailored sports jacket, 1960s pegged pants, monogrammed French cuffs and a genuine linen handkerchief tucked in his back pocket to blow his nose, which he did, loudly and often. He was trim, tall, almost 6'1," and strode with purpose and energy.

I soon learned there was a whole lot more to this Fancy Dan. The guy had insatiable curiosity, astute observations, fierce opinions and a combative passion for excellence. Oh, and a highly developed intellect. He was so intense that getting into a spirited discussion with him on most any subject was like getting into a knife fight in a telephone booth.

I liked his can-do attitude—and access to deep pockets to back it up. As I got to know him better, it was uncanny how we shared so many keen interests: Sports, politics, Seagram's V.O., competitiveness and a robust admiration for bright, beautiful women. Our favorite ice cream was Breyers butter almond, and our go-to eateries were DiNardo's for hard shell crabs in Wilmington and steak pizzaiola at Jimmy's Milan on 19th Street.

And ketchup: Neither of us could eat a steak, no matter how USDA prime, without a hearty dose of good old Heinz. In fact, before trying a new restaurant, he would have someone call to make sure they had ketchup. At a fancy restaurant in Paris, I'm told, where the chef didn't allow it, he slipped the waiter an American C-note to duck out and buy a bottle.

Another time, on vacation together with our wives in Acapulco, he attempted to communicate with the waiter and conjured up: "Senõr . . . uh, sauce de la . . . er, tomato, por favor," Lao, the savvy native waiter listened, then said, "Ketchup? Sure, Boss, right away!"

How much do I love ketchup, or as the *Bon Appetit* crowd spells it, *catsup*? So much that my wife still tells people that when we were dating 100 years ago, she creatively served me beef flambé with red wine, mushrooms and apricot brandy, "and he doused the flame with ketchup!"

Even now, when she makes a mouth-watering prime meat dinner, which she insists doesn't need catsup, or ketchup, I plead, "I'll just keep it near in case of an emergency."

So, the question I get a lot is, how did Ed Snider and I meet? And how did I get into sports? I talked earlier about that as part of the Snider-Wolman feud.

As you may recall, I was a 28-year-old hot-shot reporter for the *Philadelphia Daily News* covering City Hall and area politics and was introduced to Ed by Philadelphia Eagles owner Jerry Wolman.

I got to know the boyish, fun-loving 37-year-old Wolman in early 1964 when the Eagles got into a bare-knuckled dispute with the petty and political Mayor James H. J. Tate over the Eagles' signed, exclusive professional football lease to play in the proposed Veterans Memorial Stadium. Digging around, I discovered that Tate was courting a rival American Football League franchise to share the stadium with the Eagles and Phillies. There were whispers that Tate or those close to him might benefit from such an arrangement, though it was never proven.

I interviewed Wolman a few times and he told me, "You've got to meet Ed Snider," his right-hand man who ran the Eagles organization as executive vice president and treasurer.

Wolman was a dynamic DC developer reportedly worth $36 million. He had shocked Philly movers and shakers in November 1963 by outbidding them at $5.5 million to win the franchise. Tate thought he could strongarm Wolman into accepting the rival team, sneering that this was how things worked in his town. Wolman was a friendly, low-key guy, but not one to be fucked with.

Going from a broke, bleak life in down-on-its-heels Shenandoah, PA, to a counter job in a paint store in the nation's capital, to developing major apartment and office buildings—some at the request of President John F. Kennedy, who personally enlisted Jerry to help create a prestigious Pennsylvania Boulevard—Wolman was a self-assured developer and very much his own man.

As the story goes, Wolman and his wife, Anne, earlier decided to quit Shenandoah, pick up a hitchhiker and head wherever the passenger was headed. Luckily, the hiker was a normal bloke thumbing toward Washington and wasn't the Schuylkill County slasher.

Wolman was new in town when Tate and his cohorts summoned him to City Hall and laid down tough new terms:

1. The Eagles, despite a signed exclusive football lease, were going to have to share the proposed city-owned stadium with an AFL team, in addition to the Phillies baseball team.
2. His rent was being doubled.
3. The stadium, long planned for South Philadelphia, was now going to be built over the Pennsylvania Railroad tracks at 30th Street Station and be managed not by the city but by Madison Square Garden Corp., which apparently had been behind the AFL team ploy.

Wolman said he was handed the new lease and told to sign it on the spot, or the city would force him out of Franklin Field by pressuring the University of Pennsylvania, his home field's landlord. Failing to reason with the mulish Boss Tate, you'll recall, Wolman said he walked out of City Hall "pissed," and in a 10-minute phone transaction bought 55-year-old Connie Mack Stadium, the Phillies home, which the ball club previously had sold to New York investors. Then he called Phillies owner Robert R. M. Carpenter and made a deal to share the old ballpark at 21st Street and Lehigh Avenue until they could construct their own stadium.

Outfoxed by Wolman and outed by my news stories, Tate caved and ended the backroom negotiations.

So now I get to know Snider better, this hardwired package of ambition, foresight and passion, over lunch at Bookbinders in Olde City, dinner at the Hunt Room in the Bellevue Stratford Hotel on Broad Street and drinks at the intimate Bellevue Court, a gem tucked behind the hotel. I make sure, as a journalist, to ethically split all the tabs—which hurt my wallet a lot more than his.

I introduce him to District Attorney Arlen Specter, Phillies manager Gene Mauch, pitcher Jim Bunning and influential U.S. Senator Hugh Scott, and host him in the press box atop old Garden State Racetrack in Cherry Hill, NJ. He offers me jobs—in the Eagles' front office, or running the Yellow Cab Company, which Wolman buys, or at the just-born NFL Films, which Snider and Wolman are backing.

But "Front Page Lou" is having too much fun covering the city to get stuck in an office job, at least until Ed makes me an offer I can't refuse.

"We're applying for a franchise for Philadelphia in the National Hockey League," he confides one day in early 1965. "If we get it, we have to build a new arena in Philly. Does that interest you?"

Whoa! Now this is literally a whole new ball game. I tell Ed if they get the franchise, which would be a long shot for hockey-barren Philly, despite the impressive credentials of Wolman, I'll come aboard. We leave it at that.

Several weeks later, he calls me with the news.

"We got it. You in?"

I don't hesitate. "I'm in."

And so began a rollicking journey spanning the next half century as best friends, co-conspirators, confidants and creators of exciting projects—and having a damned good time doing it all.

As close as we were, and as much as we accomplished together, our personal relationship technically didn't transcend an owner-employee basis. I never asked for a contract, and none ever was proffered. The former was the result of my independent streak, not wanting to "be owned." In hindsight, I should have pushed for a piece of some of the successful entities I helped create or shape. But that vibe just wasn't there at the time. The companies were still young.

This was short-sighted on my part, and it would have been nice to have had a boss like Wolman, who made millionaires out of many of his key guys, including Ed Snider. After I left the organization in 1980, Snider began issuing valuable pieces of equity to key execs, admitting in an interview that he may have been too hard on past aides and now saw the value of locking them in with pieces of the pie, which grew exponentially over the years.

Unfortunately, Wolman went broke being overly generous, and I believe Ed took that to heart in playing it close to the vest—sometimes, a little too close and a little too controlling for my comfort.

One incident occurred when I was running the Spectrum and a friend told me his radio station was for sale. He said if I referred the buyer, he would give me a commission. I mentioned this to Ed in passing and he wigged out. He called my friend and ripped him a new one.

"I've never been screamed at like that in my life, even as a kid," my friend told me after he got the call.

"No one pays my employees but me!" he said Ed yelled over the phone. "I'll decide what they get!" I didn't care. In those days I had unbridled confidence and felt I'd never run out of bullets.

Working with Ed was fun and exciting but often exhausting. He loved pretty much everything I did, but that is not to say it was easy. He was a demanding, hard-nosed perfectionist who never let up. If you said something was going to happen or be completed by a certain date or within a budget, it damn well better be so. And even so, there could be criticism.

Ed didn't always remember me giving him a heads up about a particular project I had launched, which would lead to annoying carping and second guessing. Finally, I started documenting things in memorandums, which I hated doing because I've never been a CYA guy. As brilliant as Ed was in so many areas, this was an issue that frustrated many of his execs over the years.

There was no HR department or employee protocol guide, so I basically took Fridays off in the slow summers and maybe one week in the winter to go someplace warm, often with Ed and our wives. I went nearly 15 years without taking a sick day, mainly because I was healthy and loved what I was doing. But once, when I took a four-day July Fourth weekend, he called from Maine to pointedly ask if I "had retired." I was pissed, but that was Ed being in control.

As any great leader, he had his moments, but supported me implicitly in many of my initiatives, even over the objections of some of his conservative legal and financial advisers. He bailed me out more than once when I went too far or fucked up royally. He had my back, and I'll never forget that.

I had his back, too, and he knew it. There was a mutual respect. There were no lectures, no woulda shouldas, no blame game. And no recriminations, other than maybe he wouldn't speak to me for a few days or he'd "forget" to include me in the annual team picture, which is why I'm in some and not others in the early years.

Ed was a damned fine businessman. He took care of the finances with clockwork precision. No matter whether things were good or bad, everyone always got paid on time and vendor invoices were satisfied promptly, even from our spare beginning. His credit on the street was golden. His reputation was peerless. John Bunting, Jr., the chairman of First Pennsylvania Bank, told me that he could set his calendar by the arrival of the Spectrum's check to pay off our jumbo loan by the first of every month.

Ed was always in motion, either in long meetings, on lengthy phone calls or traveling. He did breakfast confabs, business lunches and dinner meetings—sometimes seven days a week. His family rarely saw him at home for dinner. Nobody would outwork him or outthink him. Other NHL owners recognized his skills, and he quickly became one of the NHL's power brokers, a pivotal force in expansion, media rights and player bargaining.

He was born for combat and driven to succeed. As hard as he drove his key people, he never let himself off the hook, literally rolling up his sleeves and working shoulder to shoulder with them.

There was one instance of a monumental fuckup in the Flyers box office in our fourth or fifth year in business, a few scant weeks before the home opener. I don't recall what all went wrong, but season tickets hadn't been mailed out, individual tickets weren't ready for sale and the whole manual system was in a state of disarray with tickets piled all over the box office and on the floor. This was a disaster in the making. He pulled me aside. "Keep an eye on everything Flyers while I sort things out," he said.

Quickly sizing up the mess, Ed had all 550,000 tickets (14,000 seats times 37 home games) boxed up and moved into his office. Within hours, his office became the box office as he, his secretary, Carol, and one of the more efficient ticket guys worked nearly around the clock separating and organizing each games' ticket manifest. For three days, deliveries of pizza, hoagies, cheesesteaks, sodas and coffee went in, and full ashtrays and empty containers came out.

They organized, packed and addressed envelopes for season ticket orders and partial plans and rushed them by the hour to the main post office at 30th Street. Public ticket announcements finally were made and single-game tickets for the first handful of home games went on sale at the front of the Spectrum, where fans eagerly queued up.

What a Herculean effort, led by this resourceful, disciplined guy! There was a job to do—not exciting, but vital—and he got it done. The press and public never heard about it, nor did it distract from the rest of the organization. No one outside was the wiser regarding this near-catastrophe.

Ed went home and stayed in bed for nearly two days. He was exhausted and running a fever. On the third day, he walked in about noon, his face pale and eyes red.

"Ok, what'd I miss?" he asked.

He was back!

That was him: A workaholic. A perfectionist. A powerhouse who could size up a situation in a flash, ask incisive questions and make critical decisions, most of which were the right ones. He didn't dick around, mull things over or look for a consensus. Never saw anyone sharper on two feet, especially in confrontations.

Like all of us, Ed had likes and dislikes, but when he didn't like something, you knew it. He was a moody, emotional guy. That came with the brilliance.

I remember leaving Frankie Bradley's restaurant on Filbert Street in Philly one night with Ed, his first wife, Myrna, and his folks, Sol and Lillian. Ed, whom his mom had nicknamed "Tadpole" when he was little, was unhappy about something or other. His mother listened to his rant, shook her head and quietly said to me, "I don't know where he came from!"

I had many ideas on making the Flyers and Spectrum zing, some solid, some zany. We had an unspoken arrangement that I could pretty much call the shots on my initiatives, but I knew enough to run the more risky or costly ones by him. If I couldn't shoot down his dev-il's advocate barrage, I'd try other ways to accomplish my ideas, by getting a sponsor to underwrite them or tamping them down from just plain wild to let's hope we don't get arrested.

I dubbed us Flash & Cash. If I was a riverboat gambler, Ed was a card counter. I doubled down, he cut the odds. I was a swaggering Sagittarian. He was the cautious Capricorn.

■ ■ ■

I had a ball getting the Flyers off the ground in 1966 and '67, but jumped at the chance to run the troubled Spectrum as well in 1973. The building had been operating on a shoestring after falling into court-protected Chapter 11 after Jerry Wolman went belly up. Ed and his brother-in-law Earl Foreman successfully bid to take it over by meeting a less qualified rival's offer to pay off creditors 100 cents on the dollar.

The building needed spit and polish and a load of fresh thinking.

As you know, one idea I had was to stage major boxing at the Spectrum to fill dark Monday nights. I convinced Ed to "guarantee" $1 million by laying out a plan to stage a year of Monday night fights, each with a purse of $20,000.

Another initiative was to add more seats to the building. The Flyers and concerts were drawing at capacity. More seats meant more revenue from tickets, sponsors, parking and concessions—hefty numbers. I already had filled every nook and cranny of the building, shoe-horning in seats wherever there was space, but we could use a whole lot more to satisfy demand. Could we add a third level, I wondered?

When our architects at Chicago's Skidmore, Owings and Merrill confirmed that the existing columns to the roof could support a new tier of five or six rows, I got busy. Armed with a vivid rendering of a third deck in place and charts full of facts and figures supporting the project, I went into Ed's Spectrum office and told him all about it.

Ed jumped at the idea but, of course, had to be convinced it would work. How much is it going to cost? How many seats will it add? What about sightlines, how much would we charge for tickets, how long would it take to build, do we need to close the building, when do we break even, how much will we gross a year and net after five years, factoring in season and single-game ticket hikes and—phew—how many more ushers, security and cleaners do we have to pay?

You don't go into a meeting with the surgically precise Ed Snider without being fully prepared—unless you enjoyed having your balls handed to you. The questions would come hard and fast, like bullets ripping holes in your story. If you didn't have your shit together you quickly were headed back to your office with your head down. This was a Snider trait, whether you were his driver, a Congressman or family.

I had a pretty good instinct for anticipating the good, the bad and the ugly of how things might play out and had most of the answers. I would grill myself before heading into the fire. I knew enough about

Ed Snider to hit his sweet spots and handle the "what ifs." With him, you needed to see around corners.

"Whaddya think?" I said, finishing the third deck pitch.

"I love it," he said, "Now go sell it to Joe and Fitz."

I hated that part. Gotta go sell it all over again!

Joe Scott and F. Eugene "Fitz" Dixon, Jr. were minority Flyers partners. Scott was the active president of the team who had bought out the personal early stake of Aramark President William Fishman.

Fishman had rescued Snider with an 11th-hour cash infusion of a half million by pledging his personal company stock for a loan when Ed was scrambling to raise the $2 million expansion franchise fee. Wolman's financial collapse had left Ed pretty much on his own to come up with the bulk of the money. Fishman eventually opted to sell back his 25 percent of the Flyers, since he had jumped in solely to protect his company's multi-million-dollar investment in fronting and equipping the Spectrum as the arena's exclusive concessionaire. Scott paid off Fishman's bank obligation and became a part owner of the Flyers.

"Without Bill Fishman," Snider often said, "I would've been toast! He saved the Flyers."

Joe Scott was a robust, old-school Philly businessman with a large ruddy face and a healthy mane of white hair. He wore thick-rimmed black glasses, a camel hair overcoat—and often a scowl. The pockets of his great overcoat, inside and out, were stuffed with Flyers brochures, ticket forms, comp tickets and team souvenirs. He wasn't just an investor, but a force for good, introducing hockey to the monied Main Line crowd and to influential corporate leaders.

Joe had made most of his fortune running the world's largest beer distributorship, Scott & Grauer of Brewerytown, in my old neighborhood. He made Ballantine Beer a household word, sponsoring sports on radio and TV, especially Phillies games, with the familiar three-ring sign and name emblazoned atop Connie Mack Stadium scoreboard in huge letters.

Joe had sold his interest in the beer distro company at age 58 and was not enjoying retirement. When the opportunity to invest in the Flyers came along, his wife, Pat, insisted he not only buy in, but go back to work—for both of their sakes.

He and Ed got along just fine. Joe marveled at Ed's obsessive, hands-on style and drive and Ed left Joe alone to do his thing, chiefly overseeing season ticket sales, novelties and riding herd on the staff's expense accounts. I don't think he and Ed ever had a cross word.

I had a terrific relationship with Joe and learned a lot working with him. He seemed to see in me a younger version of himself, a Philly kid making it on his own. I respected his vigorous style and he liked the way I handled his and Ed's projects. Joe was 60 and I was 30—and he wore me the hell out.

If Joe Scott liked you, he liked you. If he didn't, watch out! Chuck Bednarik, the Penn and Eagles football legend, once kidded Joe about his weight. "Joe, looks like you've put on a few pounds," he observed good-naturedly in greeting Scott at an event one day. Joe cut him off with a dagger look and never spoke with him again. At dinners and games, Joe just would ignore Concrete Charlie's outstretched paw.

Most days, when Joe arrived, he'd ask me what kind of a mood "Mt. Vesuvius" was in. We all had witnessed Ed's eruptions when things didn't go right, or the way he thought they should have. If I told him that Ed was breathing fire, he'd wait a few hours before going in to discuss something—or worse, he'd send me in on his behalf.

Mr. Dixon, the blueblood, was another story. "Fitz" Dixon was a preppy Philadelphia socialite and heir to the vast Widener and Elkins family fortunes whose life revolved around charitable and civic causes. He sat on many boards and lived on the sprawling gentle-man's Erdenheim Farm abutting northwest Philadelphia, where he raised prized Black Angus cattle and show-worthy flora. He was owner of famed show jumper Jet Run and other world-renowned horses, he bred racehorses, and he championed the Devon Horse Show, whose Dixon Oval was named for him. His forebears had parlayed their Philadelphia trolley car fortunes into helping found both U.S. Steel and American Tobacco Co. In 1965, Fitz was one of the wealthier peo-ple in the United States, worth an estimated $300 million, nearly $2.5 billion in today's dollars.

The prissy "Fitz" was not in the least Ed Snider's type of guy and was in the picture due to his sub rosa purchase of 25 percent interest in the Flyers from team president Bill Putman after Bill's relationship with Snider had gone south over Ed's unilateral firing of GM Bud Poile.

One day, Ed got a letter from Fitz, demanding to know what Ed was going to do about "the debacle" of all the brawling the Flyers were doing on the ice.

Ed, his face serious as a heart attack, showed me the letter. "How do I reply to this?" he asked through clenched teeth.

"Tell him," I said, "if it keeps up . . . we're just going to have to install more seats."

Ed buzzed his secretary and gleefully dictated that exact message. Then he crumpled Fitz's letter and threw it in his waste basket.

Fitz never mentioned it, nor challenged Ed, after that.

Bill Putnam had been a young, rising banker at Morgan Guaranty in New York who helped Wolman and Snider craft the deal to win the hockey franchise. Bill was a handsome, pleasant and capable administrator who made the fatal mistake of aligning with the team's prickly general manager, Bud Poile, against Snider.

Snider fired Poile for trying to undermine him by disparaging him around the team and the league. Poile, a brusque hockey lifer, still was yoked to a time when owners should be seen but not heard, and resented Snider's sticking his nose into the hockey operations, especially after Ed and I relocated from center city offices to Flyers' quarters in the bowels of the Spectrum in 1969.

Things that had been simmering came to a boil the night of December 17, 1969, following a Flyers–Rangers 2–2 tie at Madison Square Garden, when Poile chewed out Harlan Singer, the Flyers radio-TV producer, for airing a Snider interview piece between periods back to Philly viewers. I was with Singer, about to board the team bus back home, when Poile confronted him: "I'd better never see that son of a bitch on a game again if you want to keep your job."

First off, I was Singer's boss and Poile had zero authority over him. I didn't tell Poile how to run the team and he couldn't order around my staff. Second, Poile's belligerence was damaging and unacceptable, as other Flyers personnel couldn't help but hear it.

Nearly all the players and staff already had boarded from a squad that included captain Ed Van Impe, Gary Dornhoefer, rookie Bobby Clarke, Bernie Parent, Doug Favell, Simon Nolet and Andre Lacroix. We just were waiting for the trainers to load the dirty uniforms and equipment to shove off back to Philly. I told Poile he was out of line, but he just climbed aboard and took his customary front row seat across from the driver next to an uncomfortable Coach Keith Allen.

Ed was traveling, so it wasn't until early evening the next day that I reached him by phone at his home and told him what had gone down. Quiet for a moment, he asked, "What do you think I should do?"

"You can't let this shit go unanswered," I said. "Too many people heard him put you down—again."

"Come over," he said. "I want to understand exactly what was said and how."

It took me a half hour to get to his home in Wynnewood off City Avenue. We talked for another half hour, after which he called Singer, who confirmed the ugly confrontation, word for word.

Shaking his head in disgust, a grim-faced Ed said, "I'm going to call Bud right now and if he doesn't have a decent explanation, I'm going to fire his ass!"

I recall Poile, his wife Margaret and family—including a son, David, who went on to become a successful NHL general manager—lived in Bala Cynwyd, where he answered the phone. It probably was close to 10:00 p.m.

"Bud, Ed Snider . . . I just heard something really disturbing that I've investigated and believe is true."

I don't recall Poile's reply, but heard Ed curtly tell him, "We can't work together anymore," and that he was being dismissed "effective immediately."

A defiant Poile, most likely thinking that Putnam would cover him, shot back that he'd "be in the office at 9 o'clock tomorrow as usual."

"Don't bother," Ed said. "You're fired!"

Snider was about to hang up when Margaret grabbed the phone and asked Ed whether he was going to live up to Poile's contract.

"His contract will be honored," Ed replied quickly, and hung up.

On the spot, I hand-wrote a short statement that Poile had been fired "for irreconcilable differences" and called our public relations director, Joe Kadlec, to clue him in, then dialed beat writers John Brogan at the *Evening Bulletin*, Ed Conrad at the *Daily News*, Chuck Newman at the *Inquirer* and Ralph Bernstein at Associated Press. Joe reached out to his contacts at United Press International and the Philly radio and TV stations.

Snider took a lot of heat for the move. Firing a GM was practically unheard of at the time and canning him just days before Christmas was bad. But Ed rode it out, religious to his principles of separating emotions from running a business, whether employees, friends or family.

Ed was mostly intractable but knew when to be flexible. Here are a few examples:

One afternoon he bolts into my office, almost like Kramer on *Seinfeld*, and quickly closes the door.

"Lou," he says, "We got a problem!"

"We?"

"You gotta help me out. My secretary just told me she's going to marry one of our players."

Like most sports organizations, we had an ironclad policy that females in the front office could not date players because confidential information such as salary negotiations, possible trades or roster moves could roil a locker room. This still is sacrosanct with many teams to this day.

Several months earlier, I had fired a Flyers secretary for that very reason, though she actually seemed to be "dating" several players. Maybe if she had been—uh—"dating" the executives, I coulda cut her a break. Just kidding, of course.

"Christ, Lou, I can't lose her. She's been with me for years and is too important to me."

I thought for a moment.

"Not a problem," I said. "She's not dating the player, she's marrying him. That's totally different."

"Wait, that's right, she's marrying him. You're a fucking genius!" he said.

You had to be fast on your feet if you wanted to stay two steps behind Ed Snider.

That was before HR was created. "Human Relations" changed office behavior big-time, with employee manuals and lots of do's and don'ts protocols.

You have to understand that the sixties and seventies were a different era. Free love was in and traditional values were out. The sexual revolution was in full swing. The stuff that went on in many offices in those days would make *Mad Men* look more like *The Brady Bunch*. It was a time of miniskirts, burning of bras, office hanky-panky—and maybe even a toke or two during happy hour. Wide acceptance of contraception gave release to inhibitions.

At the core of sexual liberation was the radical concept that women, too, enjoyed sex and had needs, perhaps outside the boundaries of an existing relationship. Temptation was everywhere and few of us were candidates for "Husband or Wife of the Year."

Theaters showing erotic films proliferated, and VCR tapes of *Deep Throat*, *The Devil in Miss Jones* and other sexually explicit videos could easily be rented. The secretaries at the Spectrum knew I had a copy of *Deep Throat* and asked if they could watch it on the VCR in my office. I told them I didn't want to know anything about it, but that I was going to be out of town for a few days and that they might just find the tape hiding in plain sight in one of my drawers. I heard that six or seven of the ladies soon enjoyed a closed-door matinee.

Another example of Ed's flexibility in business occurred one day when he was asked to drop by the conference room to sample a new concession-stand pizza.

Ed took one bite. "Worst pizza I ever tasted!" he said. "Why are we doing this?"

"They're paying us $100,000 a year sponsorship," came the answer.

"Best pizza I ever tasted!" he said, and quickly left the room.

One thing you learned about Ed was that when he wanted answers, you gave him answers—even if you didn't have them. And you just made fucking sure they were the right answers.

We had undertaken a major project relocating the concession stands to the outside of the building and facing in, so the old food and beverage stands could be converted into luxury suites. Following completion, one of the contractors, Pangborn Electric, still had its trailer on the scene for several weeks servicing checklist items. Ed and I were returning to the building after a quick lunch at the nearby Penrose Diner. With us was Spectrum sales director Ivan Shlichtman. Ed spotted the trailer.

"When is that thing going to be the hell out of here?"

"June 11," I answered without hesitation, a date about two weeks away.

"About damn time," he said and entered the building.

Ivan, one of my closest friends, gave me a quizzical look. "And you know that how?"

"Because," I nodded quite seriously, "you're going to get on the phone and tell them to get that piece of shit out of here by then."

"Pangborn June 11" became our inside joke, the go-to phrase when Ivan and I didn't have a ready solution for something.

Having an explosive boss is like riding a bronco. To stay on, you have to know how to ride it. Some tones of voice or black moods you don't mess with. You ignore it, manage it, or challenge it at a more opportune time. Which is what I did on more than one occasion.

Ed and I saw eye-to-eye on most things, but we did have a couple of moments.

Hosting a weekly meeting with my Spectrum VPs of marketing, security, operations, bookings and finance, I was more than surprised to see Ed walk into my office unannounced and sit down. This was a first and didn't sit well with me because it likely meant someone had bitched to him about me. The meeting continued, albeit in a charged atmosphere, as we reviewed the past week's events of two hockey games, two basketball games and a concert.

When we finished, Ed brought up the subject of his new corporate VP, an abrasive accountant whom Ed hired away from our auditing firm to control the growing organization's finances. Ed said that the accountant didn't understand my explanation for upgrading our black-and-white scoreboard's basic software.

First of all, I didn't like this little bean-counter's pushy style and wasn't about to have him question me about a minor discretionary expenditure in a budget long ago approved. This was a putz short on stature and long on ego and looking to impress the boss.

The new VP had asked me why I would "waste money" on upgrading software when the Flyers already were selling out. Dumb, provocative question. For a few thousand bucks it allowed us to pioneer some early click-click animation. Who was he to ask about running an arena? Did I tell him how to balance his fucking books? Where was he when we were scraping pennies to stay afloat?

"Because that's how you stay sold out," I mansplained the accountant. "It's Marketing 101."

He didn't like my answer. I didn't like him.

"Why didn't he understand your explanation?" Ed asked.

"Maybe he's thick," I said.

Ed exploded.

"Fuck you!" he screamed, his face crimson.

My VPs froze. The room went still. Heat coursed up my neck, *this close* to blast off.

I set my jaw, held my breath . . . and said . . . nothing. I wasn't going to get into it in front of these guys because things could go sideways fast. An uncomfortable moment passed before Ed got up and left the room, slamming the door.

The meeting lasted only a few more awkward minutes amid a tension you could slice with a goalie's stick. They filed out wordlessly.

I had witnessed his quick temper and sometimes irrational anger aimed at others in meetings or on taut phone calls. But this was the first time I was in the line of fire. When you're the top dog, you get to bark with impunity. Who's going to bark back?

I never hesitated to tell him if I thought he was wrong or had gone overboard on some issue. He didn't always agree but respected my opinion. This time was different. No one talks to me like that and gets away with it!

Within minutes, my desk phone buzzed, the No. 1 button from Ed's office blinking impatiently.

"Yeah?"

"Lou, I'm sorry about that, but you can't put down one of my guys in public like that," he said evenly.

"Sure, Ed," I replied, "But it's OK for you to put me down in front of *my* guys."

"Like I said," he pressed on, "I'm sorry I had to do that."

"Ed, you're the boss, but if that ever happens again it'll be the end of our relationship," I said just as evenly.

He didn't reply and I hung up.

We didn't talk for several days, taking pains to stay out of one another's way. I figured I could always get another job. He isn't going to get another Lou Scheinfeld.

Almost a week later, that No. 1 button blinked.

"Want to talk?" he asked.

I would have chewed off my right arm before making the first move. That's just me. Ed was the bigger man, and it wasn't the only time he extended the olive branch to end one of our impasses. We thrashed it out in his office, went to dinner and got happily shit-faced.

Before I left the organization, I made peace with the numbers guy who had bugged the shit out of me. He met a lovely young lady who inspired him to take Werner Erhard's "est" program, which teaches you "to transform your ability to experience living so that the situations you have been trying to change or have been putting up with clear up just in the process of life itself." In other word, take a class that makes you not be such a dick! He changed, they married, and I forgave him—kind of.

The only other time I experienced Ed's famed wrath was a few weeks after I left the organization in 1980 to become president of the 76ers. Ed had a hand in "selling me" to the NBA team when he heard it was looking for a new top executive, a tactic he employed to deftly ease out used-up execs. It worked out great for me, so we both were happy.

Fitz Dixon, who had sold his Flyers interest to Snider and bought the 76ers from Irv Kosloff, asked me to check into whether a proposed sports cable network rivaling Snider's PRISM would be worth considering. I went to one meeting and knew immediately it wouldn't get off the ground. I told Fitz their plan was lame and put it out of my mind.

A few days later when I called Snider to extend wishes for Rosh Hashana, he started berating me for "trying to start another sports network . . . after all I've done for you." I never got a chance to answer that I had shit-canned the proposal. He just went off, yelling and cursing.

Oy! And a happy fucking Jewish New Year to you, too, Ed!

I hung up on him. He called right back—twice. But I didn't take the calls. I was done with him.

Nearly 16 years would pass before we spoke again. It lasted until my close friend and former Spectrum president Aaron Siegel and I ran into him on Walnut Street in center city in 1996 and he warmly invited us to tour his new $210 million CoreStates Center. A week later he proudly walked us through the sumptuous arena, after which we broke bread in his private Director's Lounge, enjoyed a Flyers win in his suite and he and I eagerly began the healing process.

I should pause at this point to explain that probably 99 percent of my relationship with Ed was great. It's just that the other parts stand out because of their fierceness. But that was Ed. His style was his style, and to understand it was to understand his genius. We had enough respect and affection to battle like family and get over it— even if it did take 16 years!

Prior to my leaving the organization in 1980, it became obvious that the more Ed Snider prospered, the more politically conservative he became. Once it became an obsession, I knew it was the beginning of our end. He was leaning hard to the right and in-your-face militant about it. I was a sensible liberal, which is maybe why we had clicked for so long, balancing each other to some extent.

One day, at the end of a Spectrum senior staff meeting, he handed out a half-dozen copies of *Atlas Shrugged*, Ayn Rand's fourth and final book, decrying the evils of successful human beings expending energy to help the weak and the lazy. In other words, egoism and self-interest were necessary to ward off the moochers and looters. He told us all to make sure and read the book because this is what he believed in: rugged individualism and no-holds-barred capitalism. Years before, I had read Rand's book *The Fountainhead* and part of *Atlas Shrugged*, dismissing her philosophy as hard-hearted and elitist. I don't know what the other execs did, but I tossed my copy into the donation bin at my library.

I once heard an NFL owner of a team advise his kid, whom he had installed as VP right out of college, to keep a close eye on everyone in the organization because "It's our money and they're all trying to take it." Same thing.

Rand's book gave credence to Ed's hardening philosophy of free enterprise and the rewards of private business. Not one ever to just dip his toe into anything, he dove into funding conservative causes, including an institute based on Rand's principles.

He sought out the famously reclusive author, became friends, made speeches about her and ultimately convinced her to allow him to make a movie about the controversial 1957 novel, something she had firmly resisted for years, unable to find someone she thought could do it justice.

She believed in Ed and awarded him the rights, and he eventually had it produced in 2011, nearly 30 years after the Russian-born writer had passed away. He made it in three parts to capture its full thrust and even followed up by calling a contact at HBO to urge it to be run on the prestigious premium network. HBO, which had made the well-received *Broad Street Bullies* documentary, was only too glad to accommodate Ed Snider, even though reviews had been brutal.

In 2008, when he invited vice-presidential candidate and self-proclaimed "hockey mom" Sarah Palin to drop the ceremonial puck at the Flyers' opening game at the Wells Fargo Center, I told him it wasn't a good move—and that I wasn't a fan.

"Well, you should be!" he insisted. "She's wonderful."

It turned out to be bad luck for the superstitious owner, who would make an immediate U-turn in his car if a black cat was in the road, or step over cracks in the sidewalk and throw spilled salt over his left shoulder. Not only was he criticized for mixing politics with the team, but worse, the team lost that game and went winless through its first six, putting them in an early season hole.

Years before, at a meeting with Fred Lieberman, an early cable entrepreneur who wanted to televise the Flyers playoff games locally, Snider insisted they be available only for a premium fee. When I suggested that yanking them off free TV where they'd been all season was "unfair to our fans," Ed called me "a fucking Communist." Not angrily, but forcibly.

The cable pioneer, whom Ed respected, stared at him.

"You pay this guy?" he asked Ed.

"Yeah," Ed replied.

"You pay him well?"

"Yeah."

"Then why the fuck don't you listen to him?"

Ed knew he had overreacted, shot me a mea culpa look and we all laughed.

"Don't be a fuckhead!" Fred told him.

That killed the thought of zapping our faithful fans for a few playoff games in a year when we knew we weren't going deep.

Funny thing was, Ed loved the fact that Fred had called him "Fuckhead." In fact, when Fred called him that at subsequent private meetings, Ed just roared. Go figure.

Ed wasn't one to sit back when he felt the need to change the world or set people straight.

One of his kids spent a student semester with a host family in France, and the family's written exit review was far from complimentary. Sometime later, on his first trip abroad, he made sure to travel to that town and knock on the hosts' door.

"I told them off!" he informed me when he got back. "They don't get to say that about my kid."

I winced. But was I surprised? Of course not. This was a guy who stood up for what he believed, spoke his mind and didn't give a shit about fallout. He had unchecked control and "fuck you" dough to back it up. But props to him for supporting his loved ones—even traveling halfway around the world to do so.

I did ask him how he enjoyed Europe, otherwise.

"It was great," he laughed. "And if they ever move it to New York, I'll go back."

Ed did make many trips back to Europe over the years, on his sailing yacht, The Sintra, or on his private Gulfstream jet. He made summer sojourns to France, Greece, Spain and Italy with his four respective wives and an assortment of in-between squeezes, competing in sailing races (on racing boats) and visiting exotic islands.

Another time, he told me, one of his kid's professors at the University of Pennsylvania was disparaging capitalism. He said he met with the educator, expressed his views and doubled down by establishing the Sol C. Snider Entrepreneurial Research Center at Wharton honoring his late father, who turned a grocery store into a string of supermarkets. Ed said he funded the center to show that individuals and risk takers who started their own businesses deserved to retain the rewards they reaped.

"Growing up in Washington DC, I watched my father run the stores," Snider said. "He taught me to be the best no matter what job I did. If I had to mop a floor, it was going to be the best mopped floor ever!"

Snider always said that his career was not the result of a long-term plan. He liked to tell young people that he just applied himself when opportunity knocked and innovated as he went along. "Being free to follow your dreams, working hard and being rewarded for your labors is what life is all about."

Ed was generous with his philanthropy. In addition to heavily endowing the Snider (family) Foundation, which grants millions of dollars every year to causes in which he and his family believe, he created the Ed Snider Youth Hockey Foundation. Today, Snider Hockey provides more than 3,000 area inner-city children with free equipment and daily ice time along with homework help and a life skills program. Before his death, he made sure to fund both foundations in perpetuity with hundreds of millions to each from his estate.

"Snider Hockey is the only thing I want my name on after I pass," he told me. "Doing this for kids and for the city is my [main] legacy." At his alma mater, the University of Maryland, he created the Ed Snider Center for Enterprise and Markets to see that high-performing individuals thrive and businesses prosper. Ed had graduated with an accounting degree and passed the CPA exam.

"In my first job at an accounting firm, they sent me out to audit a guy who owned gas stations," he said. "I spent a week going over his books and business practices and had several thoughts where he could do a lot better. But he wasn't interested in making any improvements and blew me off. I decided right there and then that I wasn't wasting my time telling other people how to run their businesses. I went back to the office and quit—one week into the job."

With a partner Ed started Edge Ltd., a Washington record distribution business, from the back of their cars, supplying 45 rpm records in racks to drug stores and updating inventory weekly. Things were going well, and got even better when they won a contract to service area military bases.

"But we knew we couldn't compete with the big record companies, which were getting into the distribution business," he said, and they sold out to one of them.

Months later, at age 33 and looking for something to do, Ed was introduced to Washington whiz developer Jerry Wolman, who had just purchased the Philadelphia Eagles. Wolman, 36, thought Ed might be the perfect guy to manage the team's business while Jerry concentrated on his development business. He made Ed executive vice president and treasurer, with a big salary, a limo and a 7 percent slice of the team, worth about $350,000 at the time. It was November 1963.

Snider, wife Myrna and their four young children needed to relocate to Philadelphia and found a luxurious rancher for sale off City Avenue in Wynnewood owned by auto magnate Victor Potamkin. Said Snider, "I took one look and bought it on the spot—furniture, silverware, linens and all."

This house became an issue many years later when Wolman wrote in his book, *The World's Richest Man*, that he helped buy the house for Ed with a check for $83,000. Snider denied it, but documents that came out seemed to indicate otherwise. You know the story . . . my side, your side—and the truth.

By 1972, with the Flyers on solid ice, Snider and his brother-in-law Earl Forman felt financially confident enough to take the Spectrum out of Chapter 11, where it had been since Wolman defaulted. They told me to get ready to run the arena.

The day after they took control of the building, they fired Spectrum president Hal Freeman, the former employee who had aligned with the penny-pinching trustees and reportedly with a rival group also seeking to take over the building. I didn't feel sorry for Hal, but bumping into him leaving the building, lugging his personal stuff in a cardboard box, was painful.

"Congratulations, Lou," he said sadly, but sincerely. I felt like shit. He was way more generous than I think I would have been if my career had been interred in that box.

Hal was well-liked around town and had no trouble finding a job. Unfortunately, it was with the Philadelphia Blazers, the ill-fated World Hockey Association team that lasted one disastrous year, averaging only 2,200 fans per game, before fleeing to Vancouver. The Blazers' opening game at Convention Hall was postponed before the opening faceoff when the Zamboni machine, which didn't arrive until 8:10 p.m.—forty minutes after the 7:30 scheduled start—rumbled onto the ice and cracked it like a pane of glass.

Hal's crew had given out souvenir orange pucks to an estimated 6,000 fans. It was almost 9:00 p.m. when they finally announced there would be no game. Boos, curses and pucks rained down on the splintered ice and anyone on it, including Hal. It was Friday, October 13, 1972.

Philadelphia Inquirer writer Frank Fitzpatrick, in recalling the incident in a 2017 column, noted that four years prior to the Blazers' fiasco, Hal had been relaxing in his office at the Spectrum during a Saturday afternoon Ice Capades Show when someone rushed in to tell him that a windstorm was shredding the arena's roof.

"As for poor Hal Freeman," Fitzpatrick wrote, ". . . the curse continued."

He would go on to work for the doomed 1976 Bicentennial Commission, the now-defunct Philadelphia Atoms soccer team, the now-shuttered Living History Center and Garden State Park racetrack, which burned to the ground in 1977. The track later was rebuilt in grand style, failed and was razed for another New Jersey shopping center.

With Hal gone from the Spectrum, I moved down the hall from my small Flyers digs to his spacious but drab President's Suite. The beleaguered arena staff regarded me cautiously.

First thing I did was call in Hal's secretary, Mae, a pleasant, middle-aged woman with whom Hal had been close. I respected her allegiance and wanted to do right by her, but I needed my own team to tackle this job.

"Mae, I'm bringing in my own secretary," I said courteously. "But we're going to be expanding and you're welcome to stay. What would you like to do?" She stayed on for a while, I recall, but eventually left, I believe, to join Hal in one of his endeavors.

Next, I called in the arena execs overseeing public relations, bookings, security, finance, box office and operations, and went around the table asking how they were doing and what they needed in order to do a better job. As expected, the answers were guarded and routine, until the operations director, Frank Herbert, attempted to school me on how things worked.

"If the Flyers, 76ers, Electric Factory or any other tenant wants something, the answer is 'No! No! No!'"

Ooh-key, I thought, this is going to be fun.

"And if there's damage, like a window is broken or a toilet smashed at a concert or family show," events for which the building shared expenses and income, "we tell the teams it happened at their last game and charge *them* for it."

Wow! More fun than I could stand.

When he finished, I said, "Guess what, Frank? From now on, the answer is going to be 'Yes! Yes! Yes!' And if you can't say 'Yes,' then come to me and we'll figure out how to make it a 'Yes!'"

It was important to set a positive tone. "The trustees are gone! Hal's gone! If anyone else doesn't get it, they can be gone too," I said. "Anyone who wants to leave today will get a severance."

"This is going to be a happy place where we work hard and have fun," I said. "It's time to stop nickel-and-diming people and ripping off the teams. They're our life's blood and the reason we have jobs!

"No one else is going to be let go. You'll have the resources to grow and prosper. We're going to make this the best, most successful building in the country. And we're going to do it the Ed Snider way—first class! If you don't want to work for me, tell me now and take your severance, because if I find out later you're fucking me you'll be out on your ass—with nothing!"

No one took me up.

But on his way out, the operations boss, a former Army colonel, warned me, "Hal had an open door. If I need to see you about something, your door better be open, or I'm going to bust right in."

"You do that, Frank," I shot right back, "and it better be that fucking important!"

Funny thing was, "Dr. No" turned out to be just fine. Once he realized there was a better way to run an arena and that there was cash to back it up, he was a changed man. We worked closely and had a warm relationship.

Operations is a huge part of running an arena, overseeing event staffing, parking, security, ushering, cleaning, maintenance, concessions, the unions, building improvements and overnight changeovers from ice to basketball to concerts to circus and rodeo. I enacted many changes over the next few years, and Col. Frank Herbert carried out every one of them as a trusted and supportive ally. He was a true professional. I had great respect for him.

Ed Snider soon realized I had a good handle on things and left me alone, needing to concentrate on his baby, the Flyers, which he rapidly was turning into a cash cow.

One of the first things I did was dress up our threadbare Spectrum offices. The whole place reeked of pettiness and pessimism. The poorest South Philly family had better-looking basements. I called in our terrific designer, Mitzie Meyers Zafero, who had decorated the Snider's home and Flyers offices, and told her she had $15,000 to liven things up, plus another $5,000 for my office. And I wanted it done overnight! This overworked, understaffed crew deserved better—and needed to see it happening pronto.

"Do you have a budget for this?" she inquired, aware of my free-wheeling rep that drove our accountants crazy. "Of course not," I said. "But we have tickets to trade and there are lots of companies out there eager to be connected to the Flyers and Spectrum." That did the trick.

In two weeks, in the main areas, Mitzie had rich-looking carpeting installed, painted the lackluster office walls with colors that popped, hung lively posters of the circus, Ice Capades and concerts, and blow-ups of memorable Flyers and 76ers moments, brought in modern desks and furniture and a hi-tech phone system. It made quite a statement. And you wouldn't believe how everyone perked up.

Meanwhile, my office was large but depressing: frayed chairs and a sagging sofa, a chipped wooden desk and laminated 'wood' paneling your blind grandfather wouldn't be caught dead with in his rec room.

I asked Ed Snider not to visit me until the "after." I don't think he could have stomached the "before." In fairness, the court trustees overseeing the Spectrum reorganization were installed to run the building on MacGyver baling wire and spit until a buyer came along.

My executive digs soon got an electric blue rug, a marble oval Knoll desk, built-in cabinets and file drawers to match the rug, some Tiffany-like desk trinkets and a button under my desk to trigger the door to swing closed and lock. I had seen that in a Bond movie and went for it. What the hell, you only live once! And it was for trade, not cash.

The big wall opposite my desk was covered floor to ceiling with a smoke-gray mirror that made the office bounce. To my left, a large glass coffee table with chrome legs served matching paisley sofas, with end tables sporting expensive-looking lamps. To my right was a lighted and mirrored built-in bar, wet sink and fridge. A 100-gallon illuminated fish tank sat atop a chromed stand in front of the mirror filled with exotic fresh-water swimmers that got oohs and aahs from visitors. There's a story behind the big, impressive fish tank.

A few weeks earlier, I returned from a meeting late one afternoon and found two tiny goldfish swimming in the toilet in my executive bathroom, a prank from Ivan and others. It was a Friday and I left them there. When I got in on Monday morning, they were still there, swimming—somehow surviving the weekend in "Philly Punch." I saw these plucky souls as a symbol: succeeding against the odds. I traded some more tickets for the aquarium to give them a more deserving home. Whenever I needed a lift, I dimmed my office lights and basked in the illumination of the tank, watching them cavort with the big fish. It was inspiring. They lasted for years, as did I.

Anyway, with my office redone, I was set. Let fucking Don King or Ringling's assertive Irvin Feld waltz in here and try to push us around!

With the upbeat tone established, I reached out to a friend at City Hall to set up a private meeting with Mayor Frank Rizzo.

I knew full well that for the Spectrum to survive, we needed to book the entertainment events now held at the city-owned Convention Hall in West Philly, near the University of Pennsylvania— things like ice shows, boxing, wrestling, indoor track and concerts. I already was working on getting boxing in house.

"I'll make Frank a deal," I said to my friend. "We won't go after conventions, conferences, political rallies and business meetings and you don't do entertainment. We can't compete with Convention Hall rates that are subsidized by the city."

A few days later, he tells me the Big Bambino wants to chew on it over dinner at Frank Palumbo's, a landmark in the heart of his South Philly turf. In a quiet corner of Palumbo's legendary night club and restaurant, the barrel-chested mayor greets me with a bear hug that nearly collapses a lung, takes his seat with his back to the wall and tucks a table-sized napkin under his chin.

He starts out by telling me and one of his cronies how he came home last night from a campaign appearance and his wife, Carmella, goes off on him about a makeup smudge on the collar of his white dress shirt.

"I had just come from a TV station where they put this crappy pancake on me," he explains.

"C'mon, Carmella, I'm almost 60 years old," he says he told her. "Whaddya think I'm out there doing? I'm running for damn mayor, for Crissakes!"

We pound the table laughing.

Over several dishes, none of which are on the menu and all of which end in "ini," I explain that the building needs these events to make a go of it. We have a big mortgage, Chapter Eleven creditors to pay off, overdue maintenance and upgrades to make—and too many dark nights. By the time the tiramisu is washed down with double espressos and some Hennessey, Rizzo agrees that the city shouldn't be in competition with a private business that had invested millions to bring in hockey and build a state-of-the-art entertainment center.

"Okay, you got 'em," he says. "But I'm doing this for you, Shonefield, not Schneider!"

"Mayor," I plead, "Ed's a good guy. He put his ass on the line with the Flyers and now he's carrying the Spectrum on his back," which is not only a horribly mixed metaphor but, even for the great Ed Snider, a physical impossibility.

Rizzo says he'll get it done—and he never asked for anything in return. To boot, Frank Palumbo picked up the dinner check. It was a good night all around.

Ed Snider was ecstatic when I gave him the news. He knew Rizzo didn't like him, for whatever reason, and was wary of the Mayor's vindictive reputation.

"You better never leave me," he said.

But by 1980, our relationship shot to hell, I just wanted to get as far away from him as I could.

The final straw was when he boosted the pushy, little financial guy who questioned me about improving the scoreboard to president of Spectacor. I was senior VP of Spectacor and Ed was president and chairman. I had overseen all of Ed's operations since Day One and wasn't about to report to anyone but him. He knew it would be a breaking point for me.

I went in and told Ed flat out that I was not reporting to this "squinty-eyed schmuck." At this point I had nothing to lose because the line had been drawn. He took a deep breath, fixed the famous Snider laser stare on me and suggested I go home and take a good, long look in the mirror and think about things.

Next day, I walked into his office.

"I went home last night and, as you suggested, I took a good, long look in the mirror, and guess what? I liked what I saw!"

He didn't know what to say. So I said it for him.

"I'm out of here as soon as possible."

In a matter of weeks, he helped me out the door, recommending me to the 76ers. But first, he took me to lunch at what was then Philly's new and fanciest restaurant, off the lobby of the Bellevue Stratford Hotel, whose name I don't recall.

The meal finished, he said, "What do you want?"—meaning what did I expect for my nearly 16 years of dedication and achievement.

I was ready.

"Six month's pay and annual rights to buy my four front-row Flyers tickets."

"You got it," he said quickly, clearly relieved that I didn't shoot for the moon and make it uncomfortable for him. My salary was about $100,000 (and earning every penny), so I got $50,000 over the next six months. The tickets, on the glass, next to the visitors' bench, were like gold in the '80s. I used them for years for family, friends and business before selling the rights for $10,000 to a client who loved sitting on the glass.

Who could've predicted that an astounding 28 years after "selling me" to the 76ers, my home phone would ring on a hot Sunday morning in June 2008? And on the line from his mansion in California is 76-year-old Ed Snider looking to reunite with his 72-year-old sidekick.

What took him so long?

This time.

18

Future Memories

Building a Museum?

Philadelphia has dozens of museums befitting such an ancient city–by American standards. But there are none about sports, which is where I come in.

I've been trying to establish a world-class, national sports museum longer than I care to remember. This has been a pet project that I refuse to let die. I was, and still am, determined to make it happen.

In September of 2011, I thought it was a slam dunk. I had hosted a big meeting in the Hall of Fame room at the Wells Fargo Center. Anyone who was anyone sat around a huge square table with name cards in front of them: former Philly mayor and Pennsylvania governor Ed Rendell; billionaire Lewis Katz; Ed Snider; mega-rich developer Bart Blatstein; boxing promoters Joe Hand (Sr. and Jr.); renowned sports memorabilia collector Dr. Nicholas DePace; Baltimore developers of casinos, entertainment centers and Xfinity Live! David Cordish and son Reed; museum architects and designers—maybe two dozen heavy hitters.

I had charts and blowups for a $30 million national attraction to be built where the Spectrum once stood and next to the nearly finished Xfinity Live! It would display memories, memorabilia and dazzling virtual reality covering all major sports. Cooperstown meets Disneyland, I trumpeted.

Along one wall behind a temporary sheet of protective acrylic stood a slew of collector Nick DePace's most valuable vintage sports artifacts, part of his vast $35 million collection. We had Wilt's

Overbrook High School jacket and his NBA Most Valuable Player Trophy; Jim Thorpe's leather helmet, bible and trophy; Chuck Bednarik's 1960 Eagles uniform; the ringside bell from Philly's Sesquicentennial Stadium (later called Municipal Stadium and then JFK Stadium), used in the 1926 Dempsey-Tunney world heavyweight championship match, which was attended by 130,000 fans in a driving rain; worn and signed jerseys from Flyers heroes Bobby Clarke, Bernie Parent and Dave Schultz; Wayne Gretzky's jersey; Joe Frazier's robe and heavyweight championship belt; Muhammad Ali's robe; Dr. J's first 76ers jersey, and Jackie Robinson's 1949 uniform shirt. Great items all!

There was a gourmet spread for the "big mahoffs" complete with a chef and omelet station, Bloody Marys and mimosas. What more could they want?

Snider vowed to make it happen. Rendell said he'd raise the dough. Katz promised to bankroll it himself. It was a slam dunk and a hat trick combined.

"It's a great destination and another reason to visit the restaurants and team stores here," said Snider.

"It's the right time and the right place," said Rendell. "I'm totally committed."

"It'll bring history alive and inspire kids to achieve their goals," added Katz.

"Good job," Snider told me on the way out, later arranging for Flyers Charities, Inc., to kick in $50,000, with the expectation that the Phillies, Eagles and 76ers would do the same every year. That way, he said, the non-profit museum would have a vital, guaranteed annual income.

But hard as we tried, neither Ed Rendell nor I were able to convince the Phillies, Eagles or 76ers to match Snider's concept. And in short order, Lew Katz perished in a plane crash, Ed Snider lost his battle with cancer and Comcast Spectacor execs informed me they now had other plans for the space.

So Dr. DePace and I looked around and found a great spot on the doorstep of the Sports Complex, across the street from the Eagles' Lincoln Financial Field. We signed a lease for 20,000 square feet of prime ground-floor space, retained lawyers and designers, created slick marketing materials and announced plans for a great, new Philadelphia destination. The building had a wide loading platform out front perfectly suited for a patio where fans could gather and grab a hot dog and a soda, whether coming to the museum or an event at the complex.

There are only a couple of cities in the United States where all four major league teams play within the city limits. We've got all four playing at the same intersection! Plus the Wells Fargo Center draws big numbers for family events and concerts. Nearly nine million people come to the complex a year to attend some 400 events. If the museum got visits from one percent of that figure, it's a success.

Perfect, right?

The 76ers were supportive promotionally, and one of its owners personally contributed, as did the Snider family, along with a few other staunch believers.

But this being Philadelphia, things got political.

Seems there were old railroad tracks buried under the grass running in front of our building that at one time serviced the loading platform. The tracks were controlled by the Philadelphia Industrial Development Corporation (PIDC), a quasi-governmental agency that at first indicated it would be no problem, but suddenly reversed course.

There were forces at the Sports Complex opposed to the museum, PIDC spokesmen informed us, and said the easement to allow the public to cross the old tracks would be withheld until we obtained written approval of our project from all four teams as well as Comcast Spectacor's Wells Fargo Center.

This was totally out of line, in our opinion. Why would we need approval from billion-dollar corporations for a non-profit project on private property? Further, who the hell was the PIDC to make us jump through hoops to create a new destination for public good?

We already had spent considerable funds at this point and continued to push forward. We applied for the necessary zoning change from warehouse to public assembly use and successfully maneuvered to obtain the mandatory approvals from the district's city councilman, Kenyatta Johnson, and the neighboring Registered Community Organization (RCO).

We weren't applying for a liquor license or opening a dance hall or even starting a hockey team. The museum was for families, schools and fans looking for something to do around events besides tailgate on a zillion acres of parking lot wasteland. Our mission was to show kids what it took for their sports heroes to make it—hard work, education, dedication and wise life choices.

There are generations who never saw Connie Mack's great teams play in the 1920s and '30s, or the Eagles winning the 1960 NFL Championship, or the Phillies finally, after 97 years, winning their first World Series in 1980. How about the great Warriors NBA teams and Chamberlain's 100-point explosion against the NY Knicks in 1962? Twenty years from now, we'll need to relive the Eagles' 2017 Superbowl win over Tom Brady and the favored New England Patriots, the 41–33 thriller featuring the fabled "Philly Special" touchdown.

I knew nobody in the Sports Complex would come forward and publicly oppose our project, because there was no legitimate reason. What could they say? That we'd be a nuisance with drunks and late night noise, that we'd be competition for the fans' dollar—or that someone had a hard-on for me because I didn't go quietly into the night after museum proponent Ed Snider passed away and I was told there was no space for the museum?

I had worked for enough teams and venue owners to know that they want to own and control everything. I don't blame them. It's a competitive world and they've got big investments—and bigger egos.

But come on! We're a bleepin' non-profit looking to give fans and visitors something good, something noble, something educational. Something that doesn't exist in a sports-crazed town. The Museum of Sports would be one of the only venues in America open to the general public celebrating all major sports on a national basis. Rare memorabilia, rotating exhibits and immersive virtual reality displays would make it a must-see experience.

With approvals from the councilman and the RCO in hand, we received unanimous approval from the City's Zoning Board of Adjustment and good wishes from its chairman, Frank DiCicco, who said the sports museum was a long time coming and he looked forward to its success.

But building a first-class museum in an old, stark warehouse is expensive. We needed to raise $8 to $10 million to do a great job. You get only one chance to make a good impression, and if we didn't open with a bang, we wouldn't survive.

We knew one thing—that we couldn't count on most of the teams for any funding. We also kept getting word that "they didn't want the museum on their doorstep" and because of that, neither did the PIDC. Finally, when a potential mega-donor told us that he wouldn't contribute further because a Sports Complex executive informed him "the teams are against it," we began looking for another site.

Since then, there have been significant changes at PIDC, as its very political president moved on and a new chairman came in. But you can push water uphill only so long.

What we needed was a building that didn't require millions in upgrades, maybe a recently closed Sports Authority store or part of a shuttered Macy's. We found some possible sites, but retail rates of $30 to $50 per square foot are way too expensive for a non-profit. South Philly? King of Prussia, Penn's Landing, West Philly, the Navy Yard? Up Broad Street? Along I-95? We've looked everywhere. And we're still looking. Got feelers from New Jersey officials for sites in Camden, Atlantic City and Wildwood. Thought we had a good shot with the reopening of a big casino/hotel at the shore, but the complex suddenly was sold and the new owner wasn't interested.

The coronavirus shutdown sure hasn't helped. And will the world ever be the same? Non-profits are being squeezed. Museums are scaling back. Donors are holding off.

What's next? Pestilence, a plague of locusts? Hopefully, by the time you read this, there's a happy ending: an angel with deep pockets has stepped up and funded this terrific project.

Philly's a gritty underdog of a town. Its fans never give up. Rocky didn't.

Yo! We ain't either.

Epilogue

Far be it for me to quibble with a pretty fair writer named F. Scott Fitzgerald who famously wrote in *The Last Tycoon*, "There are no second acts in American life."

But I do beg to differ. I've had more acts than Fritz the Cat had lives.

I'm not sure to what I attribute this run of curious rebirth. Luck? Right time and place? A hard head? Probably all three. Plus, maybe, resiliency.

I've had the greatest jobs in the world: journalist, sports team exec, arena manager, political adviser, author (if you count this book).

And, for my final—er—next act, *ta-da!* . . . hopefully, sports museum founder.

Not bad for a kid from a corner store in North Philly's Brewerytown.

Now in my mid-eighties, I've had dozens of close friends and dear family bite the dust. I cringe as I read the morning obit pages, spotting familiar names and faces. Powerful CEOs, big-time politicians, my sports heroes, high school buddies, old flames.

Wait, Ted Silver just died? Wasn't he the BMOC at Temple University in '57, the one who drove a red Mercury convertible and chaired half a dozen clubs? He inherited his father's huge construction business—and literally ran it into the ground.

And how about my old classmate Howie, the athlete and brainiac we all envied who, at age 50, keeled over at dinner with a heart attack called the widow-maker? A meal to die for, someone cracked. Wasn't he the kid voted most likely to succeed in my class at Central High School, who called on me when I was president of the Spectrum to pitch me on buying a family plot at a Jewish cemetery in Northeast Philly? Which I gladly did—to help him out. He even gave me a coupon book with a two-year payout, which I think was $950, not including a gravestone.

Funny thing was, I sold it years later for a small profit after getting remarried to Vicky, the young, Irish-Catholic lass, who had no interest in spending her eternity in a Jewish cemetery hard by rumbling Roosevelt Boulevard. Being the good husband (this time around), I placed a classified ad in Philly's *Jewish Exponent*, triggering a minor bidding war among Russian Jews who were populating that area.

Polina, the buyer, met me at the cemetery office. She was a stout, sturdy babushka from Buryat who looked like she could pull a plow. She asked to see the plot, which Honest Howie swore sat in quiet dignity upon a gentle hill shaded by a gracious elm.

Armed with a faded, Xeroxed diagram from the office that looked like Bluebeard's buried treasure map, we found it—along a cyclone fence just yards from fume-belching buses and semis roaring down the road.

"Ya kuplyu eto," she said, or something like that, which I took to mean, "Sold!"

Back in the cemetery office, she counted about $1,300 in crumpled U.S. $50s and $20s and took ownership of the heavenly plot for her dearly beloved.

I mention Howie and Ted as examples of how things had changed for me, and how I have changed.

Coming from the candy store in the 'hood, across the city from public, prestigious, then all-boys Central High School, where you needed to pass a stiff test to attend, I felt socially inferior to the richer, smarter kids from homes with wide lawns and fancy cars.

I had street smarts and a quick wit but didn't know squat about French or algebra or how to conjugate a verb. I went straight from little John Sartain Elementary School, kindergarten through eighth grade, to storied Central High. Most of my new classmates had two years of junior high (now called middle school) and were prepared for Central's rigorous curriculum. I fell behind from the get-go, pulled poor grades and was ridiculed, which exacerbated my shyness.

By my junior year, I got it together, was popular and accepted. Displaying athletic prowess, I was invited to pledge to fraternities to play on their teams. I didn't have the time or interest. I wasn't into that Greek life bullshit, plus I worked after school and weekends in my parents' store.

I wasn't a great student at Temple University's School of Journalism either, and dropped out in my senior year when I realized that I was a few credits short to graduate. And at age 22, I also had a wife and baby to support. I couldn't wait to get into the real world, where I just knew I'd succeed.

Seven years of enjoying the power of the press at area newspapers did wonders for my confidence, and I realized I was sharper than any of those rich Central nerds.

So, seated among the trappings of my big office at the Spectrum, I didn't mind helping out some of my former classmates who either were handed jobs in their dads' companies or were peddling office equipment, investment portfolios or even burial plots. They had seen my name and photos in the papers with sports stars and celebrities and spotted me on TV down front at all the big games and events in town. Being in sports and entertainment is the dream of many but the realization of few.

I didn't feel vindicated, but I'd be lying if I said it didn't feel good. By now, I was self-assured and happy to share my largesse. I dispensed tickets, VIP parking and autographed souvenirs generously, whether for their families, businesses or charities.

I learned a lot from Ed Snider after 20 years at his side and 35 more as close friend and advisor.

Now, he's gone, as are many of my idols who once seemed indestructible. None of us are getting out of here alive. I guess that's what finally moved me to write this tome. It's said every time someone dies, a library burns to the ground. Imagine the treasure trove that perished with Ed Snider.

I'm happy to share what I know and learned. I don't think my own family knows the half of it. It's been a hell of a ride. And I've enjoyed almost every minute.

Regrets, I've had a few, as Frankie Boy would croon. It cost me my first marriage. And I whiffed on a few other opportunities that haunt me to this day. Here are three doozies that stick out.

First, I declined to rent the Spectrum to a guy I had never heard of who wanted to use the building for six weeks in the summer of 1974 to shoot a movie he said he wrote and starred in. He had no money and a funny name.

A few years later in the summer of 1976, I'm in Manhattan for a meeting with United Artists, one of our PRISM partners, and their VP invites me up to the firm's private screening room on Seventh Avenue to preview a little movie they had just finished. He thought it had great potential.

I sit there dumbstruck. It's *Rocky*, the movie sleepy-looking Sylvester Stallone wanted to shoot at the Spectrum. Holy shit! My Bad! It was filmed in an old Los Angeles arena with Philly exterior footage and plastered with Spectrum posters.

If that wasn't bad enough, how about me turning down a close friend who asked if I'd help him become a boxing ring announcer? I had a lot on my plate with the Flyers, Spectrum and PRISM and I really didn't think much of his chances. He was a good-looking guy with a smooth voice who could mimic anybody, but what did he know from introducing punchy pugs in gritty gyms?

Of course, my friend, Michael Buffer, made it to the top of the profession on his own, is obscenely wealthy, lives a life of luxury in Los Angeles, dates super models and travels the world for blockbuster matches at outrageous fees. He's got his own company that licenses his ingenious "Let's Get Ready to Ruummble" schtick. He's been in movies, TV shows, cartoons, comic books and more.

Am I a schmuck, or what?

Wait, there's more! This one cost me hundreds of thousands of dollars. Maybe a half-million. So here I am, president of the 76ers in 1981, and I get word that Fitz Dixon wants to unload the team. It's hemorrhaging money, not drawing well and he's tired of it all.

Fitz tells me that if I come up with a buyer, there'll be "a handsome commission." I ask around, but I don't put much effort into it because, foolishly, I'm not motivated by money. Yeah, I know, don't say it.

Anyway, my friend and accountant, Alan Smith, tells me a guy he kind of knows from tennis might be interested. Doesn't know him well, but volleys with him on occasion. Now, Alan is a nice guy, an average Joe who lives in a modest house in the suburbs, and I'm thinking not exactly the type to hobnob with someone with that kind of dough. So, me being the know-it-all, of course, I laugh him off.

A few months after I depart the 76ers in 1982, I read in the paper that Harold Katz, who made gazillions starting Nutrisystem, the weight-loss company, buys the basketball team for $12 million. My accountant politely informs me, "That's the guy I play tennis with." Oy!

A 4 percent commission on $12 million comes to about—Oh My God—480,000 bleeping dollars. Nice going, Louie!

After all of the things I bragged about earlier in this book, I wanted to share the ones that I let get away. Hey, nobody's perfect. Just ask my wife.

As you already know by now, my idol Popeye sez, "I yam what I yam."

I'm not a wealthy guy, but I'm rich in more ways than most people I know. My wife of more than 35 years, Victoria, is a gorgeous, incredible woman who not only hates to shop but somehow has put up with my friskiness and riskiness. For my 70th birthday, she got me a tee shirt that reads *I May be Getting Older, but I Refuse to Grow Up*. We've put our three wonderful kids, Alexandra, Matthew and Caroline, through college, have a new grandson and at this writing, despite the world's ills, we're all in great health.

Even better, this book is being considered by a major studio for a TV series—which could be the cherry on top!

I grew up in a little candy store, where I made sundaes. I got to run a much bigger one, where I got to make waves. My life's been one of fun and games, and I wouldn't trade it for anything. Time may have taken a few ticks off my fastball, but I think I've got enough to pitch a few more acts before the fat lady finally sings.

Stay tuned.

Many Thanks for the Best of Times. . .

Recalling people, places and things that took place over a lifetime was quite a trip in sepia. Some things came to mind easily, others needed help from friends, contacts and the internet. I interviewed dozens of people and scoured biographies and old news accounts. I have attempted to write this book honestly and with respect, where earned. I unabashedly admit to incorporating phraseology that I may have admired elsewhere. All photographs and graphics in this book, unless credited to others, are from my personal archives.

Special thanks to J. Russell Peltz for vetting my chapter on Philly boxing, and to Roger Barone, the former Spectrum changeover guy, who's become an accomplished photographer and generously offered treasured Spectrum photographic memories, which for space purposes did not make it into my book.

I've met some great people along the way, many of whom today are dear friends. The Spectrum gang was a close-knit family that worked hard—and partied harder. God, did we have a blast!

My incredible secretary, the lovely, loyal Linda Kramer DePiero, tops the list along with my dear old friend and salesman *el supremo* Ivan Shlichtman. Sadly, Ivan is gone, but happily, a half century later, I remain close with Linda and her family.

I was blessed to have the support and loyalty from so many talented colleagues, including Charlie Abel, Keith Allen, Ceil Baker, Carol Canuso, Debbie Davies, Allen Flexer, Steve Flynn, Big John Foreman, Eddie Golden, Steve Greenberg, The Joe Hands, Gene Hart, Frank Herbert, Doan Hollins, Pete Huver, Joe Kadlec, Tommy Kauffman and his wonderful wife, the late Maria Milano, Paul Levine, Fred Liedman, Kathy McGurk, Margaret Middleton, Bernie Moser, AnnMarie Nasuti, Lou Nolan, Ted Reimel, Marsha Rossi, Ed Rubenstein, Larry Rubin, Ronnie Ruttenberg, Maureen Sacks, Mich Sauers, Jay Seidman, Clayton Sheldon, Aaron Siegel, Harlan Singer, Gil Stein and Jack Williams.

Also, my talented PRISM pals, Jim and Rosemary Barniak, Joe Durand, Kip Fletcher, Hugh Gannon, Janice Gehret, Judy Haupt, Alison

Lester, Craig Snider, and my son, Michael Scheinfeld. Plus the Electric Factory crew, Lee Johnson Jr., Larry Magid and Herb and Alan Spivak, and, of course, great athletes and friends including Billy Barber, Leo Carlin, Harold Carmichael, Wilt Chamberlain, Bobby Clarke, Doug Collins, Billy Cunningham, Gary Dornhoefer, Julius Erving, Ron Jaworski, Bob Kelly, Andre Lacroix, Bernie Parent, Mike Quick, Don Saleski, Dave Schultz and Joe and Jimmy Watson.

My apologies if I missed someone. I love you all—well, most of you.

More than a few of these people were friends I recruited to join me on this improbable adventure. Most signed on in the lean years when we didn't know whether we were going to make it—and didn't care. We just rolled the dice and hoped not to crap out. We believed in Ed Snider —and in ourselves. From deep in the belly of that brick bunker, we created one of the nation's most acclaimed sports and music meccas, known as America's Showplace.

We busted our asses putting in long hours and weekends, laughed a lot, cried a little, fought on occasion—but always, always kept the train rolling. Several of us continued to meet regularly for lunch or drinks before the pandemic, stayed in touch remotely, and, after vaccinations, are resuming getting together.

Now, in the winter of life—or, as Ed said, at that five-yard line—I love recalling those crazy, hazy days and joke about how I worked my way up to a basement in South Philly. People continue to reach out and thank me for kindnesses I afforded them when they were kids or for their families, something I always enjoyed doing. Being in a lofty position isn't worth much if you don't share it.

I'll wrap up this up with an anecdote about one of my closest Spectrum buddies, a longtime friend who rose in the organization after I moved on.

He told me, "Lou, anything you need, you've got."

A few years later, I called him for a couple of tickets for my kids to a big concert, and he said he was sorry, but it was sold out.

Ouch!

I told him patiently that no event is ever fully sold out, suggesting there are always ways to find a seat or two.

"Oh," he said airily, "educate me, please."

"Okay," I posed, "If the President wanted to come tonight, would you have seats for him?"

"Of course," he replied.

"Well," I said, "he's not coming. I'll take his tickets!"

And a Final Thanks. . .

To the folks who helped make this book happen:

To Richard Sand, friend, able attorney, advisor and prolific author who four years ago got the book started and motivated me to finally sit down and start typing.

To Craig Snider for his passion and energy in getting me to reach back for so many precious nuggets in preparation for our hoped-for television drama about an arena.

To Craig's scholarly friend, Dr. James McCabe, the learned and literate Dubliner who patiently guided me in the ways of memoir telling via the miracle of international Skype and Zoom.

And to my wife, the beauteous former Victoria Jeanne Forbes, who has stuck with me through thin and even thinner. I hope she is as proud of this book as I am of her.